THE MOSAIC BOOK

OF THE

AMERICAN ADOPTIVE RITE.

IN TWO PARTS

PART I.   GENERAL INSTRUCTIONS.
PART II. THE RITUAL.

SECOND EDITION

ROB MORRIS, LL.D.

PUBLISHED UNDER THE AUTHORITY OF THE SUPREME
CONSTELLATION OF THE AMERICAN
ADOPTIVE RITE.

Cornerstone Book Publishers
Photographic Reproduction
2018

N E W   Y O R K
J. B. TAYLOR, V. E. GR'D SEC'Y, 335 BROADWAY.
1 8 5 7

The Mosaic Book of the American Adoptive Rite
by Rob Morris
Introduction by Michael R. Poll

A Cornerstone Book
Published by Cornerstone Book Publishers
Copyright © 2018 by Cornerstone Book Publishers

Cornerstone Book Publishers
New Orleans, LA

First Cornerstone Edition - 2018
Photographic Rendering of the 1857 Edition.

www.cornerstonepublishers.com

ISBN-13: 978-1-61342-316-5

MADE IN THE USA

Table of Contents

PREFACE TO THE SECOND EDITION

The favorable reception given to this beautiful system of Adoptive Masonry, at home and abroad, has encouraged its originators to prepare a second edition of the Mosaic Book. A few changes, to render the work more available in practice, have been made. These consist in substituting words for symbols, and omitting all allusions to part third, which has not been found necessary.

Introduction to the 2018
Cornerstone Edition
by Michael R. Poll

It has been my experience that there are a few hot button topics within Freemasonry. These would be subjects that quickly generate a good bit of emotion with many Masons. One such subject is if the Volume of Sacred Law can be removed from the altar of the lodge and the lodge remain regular. Most say no. Another subject is if women can become Freemasons.

Rob Morris, the creator of the Order of the Eastern Star, takes us right up to the line of female Masonry with his *The Mosaic Book of the American Adoptive Rite*. It is, of course, not actually female Masonry, but what exactly is it and why was it created?

One of the so-called landmarks that is accepted by every recognized Grand Lodge of which I am familiar is that a woman cannot become a Freemason. What I have not seen answered in any satisfactory manner is the simple question of why it is not possible. The most often answer given is that it is prohibited in the landmarks. But is it?

When we look at the Operative Freemasons, it is obvious that a woman might not be able to do the physical labor that was so often demanded of the Operatives. But is a ban on women an actual landmark? And if so, is it one that is valid today?

I know a number of lodges who have admitted candidates who have physical handicaps. The reason for doing so is simple; we are not Operative Freemasons. We do not need to be sound of body in order to improve ourselves with the teachings of Speculative Freemasonry.

If this landmark regarding physical fitness can be reasonably seen as unnecessary today for Speculative Freemasonry, then why is the landmark prohibiting women viewed as unchangeable? It's true that no one is doing hard physical work in Speculative Freemasonry. So why is it impossible for a woman to be a Freemason?

Maybe before we get into possible questions of why not, we need to look a bit at how we are set up as Grand Lodges. Each Grand Lodge is sovereign and independent. Yet in the United States, the sovereign and independent Grand Lodges have something of an organized understanding. While it is understood that Grand Lodges have their own particular rules and regulations, there are certain aspects of the operation of the Grand Lodges that are expected to be common and shared. For example, any Grand Lodge that would remove the Volume of Sacred Law from the altar of their Lodges would be viewed as irregular and the balance of US Grand Lodges would most likely break fraternal relations with them. The same is true for admitting women into Lodges. We may not be exactly sure as to why this is true, but I can assure you it is true.

I also believe that it is true to say that in many US Grand Lodges the personality of the Grand Master can play a good part in determining how conservative or liberal the tone of the Grand Lodge will be during his term in office. I have seen some cases where to even suggest that female Masonry exists is deemed acceptable grounds for Masonic discipline by some Grand Masters.

Some years back, I was told by a Mason, and in all sincerity, that the entire concept of female Masonry was the creation of the anti-Masons. I was told that there was no such thing, at all, as female Masons and photographs and reports of them were entirely made up. The entire subject of female Masonry is for some reason and many times very much like walking on thin ice. Simply discussing the subject can sometimes result in trouble.

I know of one case where a Mason was told point blank that if he even speaks to a female Mason, that is grounds for Masonic discipline. He was told that the same is true for any Mason who is not in fraternal relations with his Grand Lodge. When asked about a situation where one was working with someone who was a member of a lodge not recognized by their jurisdiction, the Mason was told that he should find another job. I do not believe that these sorts of extreme examples are either logical nor display proper understanding of Masonic obligations.

The Operative Masonic lodges were not civic or social clubs. They were places of business. The Operative Masons accepted construction jobs, travelled from area to area, and worked sometimes hard, difficult jobs as a profession. This was their livelihood and how they fed themselves and their families. Their reputation was everything for them. With a good reputation, they could continue to secure work. A bad reputation could mean that they did not work. If they did not work, they did not eat.

An Operative Lodge could not afford to have anyone as a member who could not do the work or was any sort of issue that could damage their reputation. A woman was not considered, on the average, capable of doing the hard manual labor that was expected of the Operative Masons. They were put in the same category as young boys, old men, or those with physical handicaps. They simply needed to be sure that the ones accepted into their lodges could do the work that was necessary.

But there could be another reason why, at that time, a woman may not be considered acceptable to become an Operative Freemason. During the medieval times, as well as other times, a woman was considered the property of her father until marriage. Upon marriage, a woman became the property of her husband. A woman, during many times in history, had no legal standing, and shared the status of her father or husband. As such, a woman would not be free to pick up and travel with an Operative Lodge if work was needed in another land. So, if we step back and objectively look at the situation, it does seem logical that if a woman had travel or physical restrictions, they would not be a good candidate for an Operative Freemason. But also objectively, it would *not* seem that a woman would be unable to provide *any* service to an Operative Lodge. In fact, some of the early accounts of Operative Masonry offer hints that women *could have* served in Operative Lodges.

In two sections of the *Regius Manuscript*, a poem dated about 1390, and considered the oldest known document concerning Operative Freemasonry, there seems to be mentioned of women as Operative Masons. In lines 41 and 42 and in Article 10, it mentions "sisters and brothers" in reference to an Operative Lodge.

Could this mean that women *may* have performed some duties for an Operative Lodge? It's certainly not definitive, but let's think about it. Not every duty performed in the construction of a building was necessarily hard physical labor. Artisans were often employed to carve the beautiful woodwork on staircases, around doorways, and other areas. A woman who was a gifted artist could certainly do this type of work.

I have read several unconfirmed reports where such women were the daughters or wives of Operative Freemasons. In such cases, they would be free to travel with the lodge, along with their father or husband. Under these conditions, it seems reasonable that a woman *could* serve as an Operative Freemason. Logic would dictate that this would not be the norm, but it would be possible. After all, the Lodge was a place of business, and their main concern was providing their customers with excellent craftsmen capable of doing the work necessary and constructing a beautiful building. If a woman was capable of doing any aspect of this work and doing so at a quality equal to or surpassing a male, then why would the Lodge not hire her? It would be bad for business for them *not* to do so.

We have very little concrete information concerning the makeup of the members of any Operative Lodge, much less all of them. The Operative Lodges, responsible for constructing so many of the beautiful structures and cathedrals in Europe for some 400 to 500 years, employed countless laborers, artisans, designers, and other workers necessary for these building jobs. With the variety of different work that was necessary, it would seem illogical that *no woman* would ever qualify for *any* of the positions during all those years.

It would also seem logical that given the times, restrictions on women, and the physical difficulty of most of the jobs, that the vast majority of the workers would be male. Since operative lodges worked independently of each other, it would seem reasonable that if women held some position in some of the lodges it could be unknown to other lodges. This would be especially true if Operative Masons, who were women, were rare and isolated cases.

While I hesitate to make any firm conclusion on if women ever served as Operative Freemasons, is clear that by the time the transition was made from Operative to Speculative Freemasonry the ban on women was established. From the earliest records of Speculative Freemasonry it is clear that women were not allowed in Speculative Lodges of Freemasonry.

When we look back at history there are three periods of time that are important for this study: the Medieval Age, the Renaissance, and Age of Enlightenment.

Historians sometimes disagree on exactly when one age faded and another began, but we may look at, for general argument, that the Medieval Age ran from approximately 900 A.D. until 1300 A.D., the Renaissance from about 1300 A.D. until about 1700 A.D., and the Age of Enlightenment following that time.

Of course, these times are estimates and just as different societies can have different customs, attitudes, and traditions, so can traits from one period vary from place to place. One area may have seemed like a society from the Medieval Age while another well into the Renaissance.

By looking at the *Regius Manuscript* and noting that it is said to have been written about 1390 A.D., this places it at the beginning of the Renaissance period. It is in this manuscript where it is suggested that men and women could have worked together in operative Lodges.

Let's look at this a bit.

The Renaissance is considered to be far more progressive, advanced in education, thought, and sciences than the Medieval Age. Certainly, the Renaissance was the golden age for Operative Freemasonry. It was during the Renaissance when so many of the magnificent European cathedrals and other beautiful structures were built by the old Operatives. But with all the advances that took place in the various societies during the Renaissance, there was one area that not only did not progress very far but actually backtracked. This area was the role of women in society and their civil rights.

Even with the medieval culture being what it was, many argue that the role of women was even more limited during the Renaissance than during the Medieval Age. During the Renaissance, women had no standing at all in society and few, if any, legal rights.

Operative Freemasonry was a profession that was dependent upon satisfied customers. It would seem logical that as society changed so did the face of Operative Freemasonry. Where during the Medieval Age it may have been impractical, in most cases, to have women as Operative Freemasons, it was not impossible. As long as the work was done properly, no one would have likely cared. But it seems that during the Renaissance, many *would have* cared if they saw a woman holding such a position.

The *Regius Manuscript* may have been reflective of Operative Freemasonry during the Medieval Age, and the absence of mention in later records and manuscripts of women in Masonry may be reflective of the change in attitude towards women during the Renaissance. But this is only an assumption. What is clear is that when Speculative Freemasonry came into being, there is good cause to view it as being modeled after the Royal Society of London.

The Royal Society, was sometimes known as the "invisible college," due to its determination to do scientific research during periods of time when to do so was very much in disfavor. To be named a Fellow of the Royal Society was, and is, one of the highest honors one could or can achieve. The Royal Society was organized in the 1600s during the height of the Renaissance. While there is no clear prohibition on women being elected to membership or fellowship, it simply did not happen in those early days. Women had one place in society and men another.

It would seem that Speculative Freemasonry's early ban on women simply followed the lead of the Royal Society and society in general. What is also very clear is that when Speculative Freemasonry was showcased to the world, it became very popular and quickly spread around the globe.

Soon after the creation of the Grand Lodge of England, Masonry spread to France. Like Masonry in England, Masonic lodges in France were for men only. But the French soon introduced a change in Masonic practice. The wives of Masons were brought to Masonic dinners and other events outside of the lodge. This was something that was not initially done in England.

What we must understand, is that with the creation of the Grand Lodge of England, Masonry may have modeled itself on the Royal Society and the Renaissance attitude, but society was moving into the Age of Enlightenment. One of the key elements of the Age of Enlightenment was women's rights. France seems to have been slightly ahead of England in this social change.

Not very long after, France introduced an even more controversial creation. While Masonic lodges were reserved for men only, there was a desire to have something in which women could participate. Lodges of Adoption were created. Rituals were written that were clearly unconnected to Freemasonry, yet had the same tone and recognition of the importance of initiation. Lodges of Adoption were not Masonic lodges, but they were the next best thing.

In his paper, *Women and Freemasonry*,[1] Dudley Wright presents us with an example of the ritual used by some of these Lodges of Adoption. The Lodges of Adoption became very popular in many areas of Europe with the exception of England. As society moved further into the Age of Enlightenment, many women asked a very simple question, "Why can't I become a Freemason?" When no logical answer was given, female, and Co-Masonic lodges were created.

For the most part, Freemasonry arrived in America much as it was practiced in the United Kingdom. This would include the same position on women and Masonry as well as Lodges of Adoption. It would seem that Lodges of Adoption were viewed by British Masonry as cleverly disguised female Masonry.

Maybe it was indeed an objection to the Lodges of Adoption themselves or the fact that the French had created it, I'm not sure. But like in England, Lodges of Adoption were not popular in the United States. Then something happened in 1850 that changed everything.

Rob Morris, a Mississippi Mason of less than five years, created the rituals for what he called the Order of the Eastern Star in 1850. Around this same time, he advanced and published rituals and instructions for Lodges of Adoption. Morris may have learned of the Lodges of Adoption from Europe or he may have simply wanted to create something for the female relatives of Masons. Regardless, the Eastern Star ritual was of the same tone as the Lodges of Adoption, meaning: religious in nature, structured in degrees, and with initiations.

Following the Civil War, Morris turned over the Eastern Star to fellow Mason, Robert McCoy. McCoy revised the rituals and the Eastern Star was not only a success but a major international success with chapters today in most areas of the world. Morris' efforts with the Lodges of Adoption never really caught on in the US.

But the movement really didn't end there. Before long there were Masonic youth groups for boys such as DeMolay, youth groups for girls such as the Rainbow Girls and Job's Daughters, and other "side orders" for women with male family members belonging to various other Masonic bodies.

By the mid-1900s, Masonry truly became a family oriented organization with various groups for any member of the family, all with Masonic themes or tones. Of course, the Eastern Star was not welcomed with open arms everywhere. To date, the United Grand Lodge of England does not allow its members to join the Eastern Star. It could be that the Eastern Star too closely resembles Co-Masonry for their taste. But bodies such as the Eastern Star as well as Lodges of Adoption only *resemble* Masonic lodges. The rituals of these "side orders" are clearly something other than actual Masonic lodges.

In the early 1800s, Masonic lodges started appearing composed of both men and women as well as solely female Masonic Lodges. Actual Masonic rituals were used in these bodies, and the clear desire was that they be viewed as Masonic Lodges. Of course these lodges were not recognized as regular, at least not initially, but they persisted.

In 1999, the United Grand Lodge of England made what many consider an astonishing announcement. They announced that two Grand Lodges composed of female Masons (The Order of Women Freemasons and The Honorable Fraternity of Ancient Freemasons) were, as far as they could determine, regular in nature, except that they were composed of women. While such a statement does not constitute fraternal relations nor is inter-visitation with these lodges allowed, it is still an amazing statement. The United Grand Lodge of England stated that these two female only Grand Lodges may be viewed *as regular*. That is an amazing statement. Of course, this statement did not include Co-Masonic lodges, nor did they lift their ban on their members belonging to the Eastern Star. But it is an amazing step.

As for male only lodges and Grand Lodges, they have been only a handful of cases where it has been reported that a woman was actually made a member of a Speculative Lodge of Freemasons. The earliest case reported is that of Elizabeth Aldworth. The date she is said to have been made a Mason is sometimes disputed, being either just before or just after 1717 in England, but that she was made a Mason does seem to be generally recognized.

The story goes that Elizabeth was reading a book in her father's home in a small room next to the library when she fell asleep. At that time, it was not uncommon for Masonic lodges to meet in the homes of influential Masons. It seems that such a lodge meeting was held in her father's large library. The lodge then began an Entered Apprentice initiation. Elizabeth woke, and hearing voices in the room next to her, she went to investigate. Upon seeing the initiation taking place, she became curious and watched for a while. Upon being discovered by the lodge Tiler, she fainted. The Lodge, being unsure of how to handle the situation, decided that the best solution was to initiate her.

There are only a handful of other accounts where women, for one reason or another, have been said to have been initiated into a Speculative Lodge. Even if all of these accounts are completely correct, it is only a small number and only because of extenuating circumstances. For the most part, Speculative Freemasonry that is deemed to be recognized and regular has been kept male only. Why? I don't really know.

There are many articles and books written on the psychology of male fraternities and the suggested need for male bonding. Gentleman only clubs have existed for generations. The apparent need for men to gather on their own, away from women, has been suggested by some psychologists as a throwback to the very early days of man when the males would gather together in hunting parties to bring home food. Whether this is true or not, instinct or not, there does seem to be a desire to keep male Masonry, male only. The exact reason why this desire exists may be unknown, but it does seem to exist.

We live in a world today that is very different than in the 1500's, 1600's or 1700's. Women are not the property of their fathers or their husbands. They are not without citizenship or civil rights. As Speculative Freemasons we do not do hard, manual labor in our lodges. Our world is also very different than the 1800's or 1900's as well. As far as technology is concerned, we have made unimaginable technological advances. What we view as every day tools of communication would be viewed as magic in the Medieval days.

But as human beings, I don't believe that we have advanced anywhere near the level that our technology has advanced. We still have the same fears, jealousies, personal dreams, and emotional frailties that were held by our medieval ancestors. I believe that we will always continue to use our mind to create amazing things, but that same mind can limit us through our emotional insecurities.

I've always heard that the male ego is a fragile thing. Are there legitimate reasons why women cannot take part in what we do in speculative lodges? Does the fragile male ego keep us separate, maybe out of concern that females will see our lodge meetings as shallow and nonsensical? Or, is there no real answer and women are not allowed in Masonic lodges simply because *that is the way it has always been done*? I don't have an answer. But, I do believe that time will provide the answer, no matter if we live to see that answer or not.

Regardless of any questions about female Masonry, or if Lodges of Adoption cross the line of acceptability, Rob Morris does provide a fascinating and very useful account of this beautiful system. From the clear standpoint of Rob Morris, this system is an effort to bring the Masonic experience into the family so that all may enjoy and benefit from a system of personal growth and advancement. Lodges of Adoption are clearly not Masonic lodges. But they still provide a moral, educational, and rewarding Masonic related experience for all who participate.

Michael R. Poll,
2018

Notes:

1. Dudley Wright "Women and Freemasonry" *Masonic Enlightenment* (New Orleans, LA: Cornerstone Book Publishers, 2006) pp. 71-92.

TAKE HEED!

Brother.

We commit this volume to your care under the covenant-seal of secrecy. It must not be *lent, sold,* or wilfully *mislaid.* It must not be *copied* in whole or in part.

Copies placed in charge of Heleon, are for the use of the Pillars and Correspondents of this Constellation, and for no other persons; and upon its dissolution or the forfeiture of its Charter, they are to be immediately returned — carefully enveloped and sealed — to the Grand Secretary [as named on the title page]. *Vide! Audi! Tace!* (See! Hear! Keep silent.)

xviii

CONSTELLATION ODES

OPENING ODE

By James B. Taylor, G. S.

Air, "Rosseau's Dream"

Gathered in our Constellation,
  From the outer world secure;
We here mingle our devotion,
  With affections chaste and pure.

Here, before our altar bending,
  Every passion we abjure;
With our aspirations blending,
  Hear us Lord and keep us pure.

From temptations, strife and danger,
  Guide and guard us with thy hand,
Fill our hearts with kind compassion,
  Bless with peace this chosen band.

Thine be endless praises given,
  God of Love, of Life Divine;
Raise us to thy throne in heaven,
  Where thy glories constant shine.

CLOSING ODE

By JAMES B. TAYLOR, G. S.

Air, "Meeting of the Waters"

Now our labors are ended, to God let us raise,
Like incense uprising, a sweet song of praise,
To Him Who redeemed us, who makes us to move,
In the bright paths of Virtue, of Honor and Love.

Ascribe to Jehovah one glad song of Praise,
Who watches our movements and lengthens our days,
Who guards us from danger, whose Spirit is nigh
To shield and support us, and check every sigh.

THE MOSAIC BOOK

OF THE

AMERICAN ADOPTIVE RITE.

IN TWO PARTS

PART I.   GENERAL INSTRUCTIONS.
PART II. THE RITUAL.

SECOND EDITION

ROB MORRIS, LL.D.

Rob. Morris

OBJECTS OF THE RITE

Chapter I

Sec. 1. The objects contemplated in the establishment of the American Adoptive Rite, are, 1, to associate in one common bond, the worthy wives, widows, daughters and sisters of Free masons, so as to make their Adoptive privileges available for all the purposes contemplated in Masonry; 2, to secure to them the advantages of their adoptive claims in a moral, social, and charitable point of view; and 3, to gain from them the performance of corresponding duties.

Sec. 2. So far as the American Adoptive Rite may succeed in these, there will be cause for congratulation, whatever amount of opposition it may encounter. No such attempt upon a National basis, has heretofore been made in America. The communication of such degrees as "The Mason's Daughter," "The Good Samaritan," "The Heroine of Jericho," etc., etc., though it may answer the temporary purpose of pleasure and amusement, does not, in any important degree, enlighten the recipients in the inherent claim possessed by the female relatives of Masons. Much less does it put them in Masonic relation with the vast brotherhood and sisterhood of the York Rite. Least of all does it influence them to the performance of reciprocal duties, without which, the Adoptive claim is but an imposition.

Sec. 3. For a wider diffusion of the Masonic scheme of teaching morality and religion by significant emblems; for inclining the influence of females towards the York Rite; for increasing social enjoyment by the Masonic tie; for ameliorating the condition of widows and orphans; and for affording increased facilities in relieving distressed travelers, the American Adoptive Rite has been framed and is now published.

Sec. 4. To secure successful results it is necessary that its votaries should apply its rules in a rigid sense; maintain its landmarks valiantly; affiliate into its bonds only those calculated, by temperament and principle, to understand and appreciate it, and work out patiently and untiringly its grand designs.

THE LANDMARKS

Chapter II

Sec. 1. The nine following principles are established as the Landmarks of the American Adoptive Rite, viz:

I. The "Star of Christ," or "Eastern Star," is the basis of the five Degrees of the American Adoptive Rite.

II. This Rite contains nothing in its ceremonies and lectures, that can afford a clue to the ceremonies and lectures of any other Rite.

III. Its lessons are eminently Scriptural and Christian.

IV. Its obligations are based upon the honor of the female sex; and framed upon the principle that whatever benefits are due by the Masonic fraternity to the wives, widows, daughters, and sisters of Masons, corresponding benefits are due from them to the members of the Masonic fraternity.

V. The control of the Rite lies in a central Head, styled the Supreme Constellation.

VI. The Supreme Constellation delegates its authority to form Subordinate Constellations respectively, to five affiliated Master Masons of the York Rite, associated together for that purpose, and responsible to the Supreme Constellation alone.

VII. An intimate periodical relationship is maintained between each Subordinate Constellation and the Central Head.

VIII. The ceremonial and lectures of this Rite are communicated by the joint instrumentality of both sexes.

IX. The entire ritual of this Rite, both esoteric and exoteric, is reduced to writing and entrusted, under due precautions, to the heads of Constellations.

To these nine Landmarks, comments are here appended:

REMARKS UPON LANDMARK I

Sec. 2. In selecting some Androgynous Degree, extensively known, ancient in date, and ample in scope, for the basis of this Rite, the choice falls, without controversy, upon the "Eastern Star." For this is a degree familiar to thousands of the most enlightened York Masons and their female relatives; established in this country, at least before 1778; and one which popularity bears the palm in point of doctrine and elegance over all others. Its scope, by the addition of a ceremonial and a few links in the chain of recognition, was broad enough to constitute a graceful and consistent system, worthy, it is believed, of the best intellect of either sex.

REMARKS UPON LANDMARK II

Sec. 3. The arcana, secrets, or esoteric portions of every Rite — and especially those of the York Rite, by far the most popular in America — have been so profoundly hidden under the sacred veil of obligation, that the most penetrating eye will fail to discover any of them in the American Adoptive Rite.

REMARKS UPON LANDMARK III

Sec. 4. To establish a correspondence between the principles of this Rite and those Masonic developments of the nineteenth century which are so eminently Christian, was considered an object of prime importance. The spirit of an ascended Saviour is pervading the workings of symbolical Masonry in America to such an extent as to influence its votaries in their selection of material and the style of their labor. This striking fact, however incongruous with Craft Masonry such a spirit may be deemed to be — is cheerfully accepted and justified in this Rite, wherein the Christian illustrations of the "Eastern Star," as heretofore communicated, have been extended in a liberal spirit, and elaborated so far as social, moral and charitable scheme will allow.

REMARKS UPON LANDMARK IV

Sec. 5. The common-sense principle of reciprocal benefits has been unaccountably overlooked in the developments of Craft Masonry in this country. It is a principle philosophical and just.

3

A woman who disregards, perhaps purposely wounds, the feelings of the Masonic fraternity, and who is negligent in rendering them encouragement in word or work, assuredly merits but little active aid from them. In this Rite, the Scriptural adage will be acknowledged, that "they who would have friends must themselves be friendly."

REMARKS UPON LANDMARK V

Sec. 6. The Supreme Constellation was, at the organization of the Rite, a self-assumed body, and will so continue during a period sufficiently protracted to test the merits of the American Adoptive Rite, and afford experience as a basis for its improvement. The Constitution and edicts of this body constitute the Supreme law of the Order, both to individual members and to Constellations; and its acts will establish precedents for the parliamentary usages, &c., of the Order.

REMARKS UPON LANDMARK VI

Sec. 7. Charters are granted to those associated under the title of Pillars, in sacred trust that the Constitution and edicts of the Supreme Constellation shall be strictly observed. To effect this, they are allowed the power plenipotentiary of selecting their female associates in office and the material to form their Constellation.

REMARKS UNON LANDMARK VII

Sec. 8. To secure the highest benefits of which the American Adoptive Rite is susceptible, and to preserve the Order from injury by imposters, a Memorial is communicated semi-annually from the Supreme Constellation to Heleon of each Subordinate Constellation and by him to the other Pillars; likewise to such Stellae and Protectors of his own Constellation as may contemplate a journey. A semi-annual of the membership and condition of each Subordinate Constellation is communicated to the Supreme Constellation, and every means practiced to sustain a vital communication between the two.

REMARKS UPON LANDMARK VIII

Sec. 9. In the organization of a Subordinate Constellation, the Pillars select five females from the number applying for and entitled to the knowledge of this Rite, and associate them with themselves under the title of Correspondents. These female officers take an active part in the ceremonial and discipline of the Order.

REMARKS UPON LANDMARK IX

Sec. 10. The publication of Tuilleurs, however novel in America, is common in France, Germany, &c., where the most sacred arcana of the various Rites are boldly committed to paper. By limiting the circulation of such works to worthy and discreet members, however, the evils to be anticipated from such a course are avoided, and a uniformity of work and instruction attained, of which, in America, Masons have no conception.

The Rituals of the American Adoptive Rite are ten in number, termed Hue Books, viz:

The Mosaic Book in two parts, embracing Preliminary Instructions, and the Rituals, Constitution and Miscellanae.

The nine smaller Books, embracing those portions, respectively, which are used by the various subordinate officers in a Constellation.

The [Hue] Books are delivered to Heleon under the following pledges:

1. That they are not to be sold, lent, or wilfully mislaid, that no portion of them is to be copied; and when not in use, that they are to be kept under lock and key.

2. Heleon will distribute those sent to him to the proper officers respectively, under the same binding pledges, who will be permitted to use them only for the purposes designated. None but Pillars and Correspondents and their legal successors can have access to them.

3. Pillars and Correspondents receiving them will commit their respective portions to memory as soon as possible.

4. The fact of the existence of such books is not to be made known to the public.

5. Upon the dissolution of the Constellation or forfeiture of its Charter, they are to be carefully enveloped, sealed, and returned to the V. E. Grand Secretary of the Supreme Constellation, as named on the title page.

6. They are always to be considered to be the property of the Supreme Constellation, to be returned when called for.

MEANS OF COMMUNICATION

Chapter III

Sec. 1. The means of communication and recognition teach the peculiar lessons of the Rite, and enable its members to recognize each other under every circumstance in which they may be placed. They are so contrived as to be easy of acquirement and use.

Sec. 2. They are of three sorts:

I. The signs, passes, emblems and technical lectures of the "Eastern Star," founded upon its traditions, and communicated without ceremonial. These are exceedingly beautiful and instructive.

II. The signs and lectures added to the above, by which it was constituted into an Order of five degrees, conferred with a ceremonial.

III. A Memorial communicated semi-annually by the Supreme Constellation to Heleon, and by him to all the Pillars and Correspondents and such of the Stellae and Protectors as may contemplate traveling.

THE PILLARS OF THE RITE

Chapter IV

Sec. 1. The individuals described in Landmark VI are reckoned as the Pillars of the American Adoptive Rite.

Sec. 2. Those desiring to take part in the diffusion of this Rite, will associate to the number of five, possessing a harmony of sentiment and purpose, and petition the Supreme Constellation in the following form:

TO THE M. E. GRAND LUMINARY OF THE M. E. SUPREME CONSTELLATION OF THE AMERICAN ADOPTIVE RITE:

The undersigned affiliated Master Masons, members in good standing in Lodges of the York Rite, as appears by the Certificate annexed, being desirous of associating ourselves in a Subordinate

Constellation of the American Adoptive Rite for the purposes contemplated in the Constitution and By-Laws thereof and no other, do hereby solicit a Charter under the title of............................Constellation, No............, to be opened at...........................

And by our signatures appended to this petition we do pledge our Masonic faith, each for himself, that should this petition be granted, we will strictly conform to the Constitutional requirements of the Supreme Constellation in all things appertaining to the American Adoptive Rite and if the Subordinate Constellation herein solicited fail to become organized, or at any time hereafter be dissolved, we agree, each for himself and his successors, that the Charter and Hue Books shall be immediately returned to your Grand Secretary.

In token whereof we have severally affixed our hands in Masonic faith.

(Signed)   ....

Each petitioner must attach his signature in his own handwriting, and append an official title in the proposed Constellation.

The avouchal of each petitioner's Masonic standing and affiliation must be in the following form:

I certify that Brother .... whose name is affixed to the above petition, is a Master Mason, affiliated in good standing in this Lodge.

(Signed)   ....Master

of ....Lodge, No............, ...

This avouchal may be made, when more convenient, by the Secretary or one of the Wardens; if by the former, the Lodge seal should be impressed. Parties unknown to the Secretary of the Supreme Constellation may afford a further identification by sending him the By-Laws of their respective Lodges, and the proceedings of their Grand Lodge. Should either of the petitioners be an official member of his Lodge, (Master, Warden, Treasurer or Secretary), he may vouch for all. Two or more petitioners, members of the same Lodge, require but a single certificate of avouchal.

Sec. 3.   The Pillars, so long as they sustain that relationship to the Order, are ex-officio members of the Supreme Constellation. They will be invited to all its Grand Sessions, consulted in every emergency, advised of every movement, and their suggestions upon all topics relative to the Rite will be studiously considered and valued. In the various publications of the Supreme Constellation their names will be enrolled, and upon their decease, their memory will be perpetuated with the respect due their services in this great and important enterprise.

Sec. 4. The Pillars associate with them five females styled Correspondents to take part in the exercises of the Rite, and the management of the Constellation. These are responsible to the Pillars alone.

Sec. 5. As responsible to the Supreme Constellation, the Pillars will report semi-annually, through Herald, the names of their initiates, the catalogue of their membership, deaths, suspensions, withdrawals, and expulsions; likewise the names and localities of visitors, if from a distance; the state of their finances; changes in the Board of Pillars and Correspondents; and general information and advice. The Charter and Hue Books, the labor and harmony of the Constellation, and the purity of the Rite are placed under their control and responsibility.

Sec. 6. To enable them to sustain their responsibilities befittingly the amplest powers are delegated to them by the Supreme Constellation, authorizing them to choose their own Correspondents; to select, from the materials offered them, proper subjects for Stellae and Protectors; nominate their own successors in office in the event of death, resignation, &c., appoint the times and places of meetings; decide on the qualifications of visitors, &c., &c.

Sec. 7. The specific duties of the Pillars respectively, are sufficiently defined in the following brief summary:

Heleon, President of the Constellation; conservator of the Charter; draws checks upon the Treasurer; and is Chairman of the Board of Relief.

Philomath, Lieutenant to Heleon, and in his absence, chief; conservator of the Landmarks, and lecturer upon the Rite.

Verger, Treasurer of the Constellation and keeper of its regalia, jewels, and other property.

Herald, Secretary of the Constellation; collection of fees and dues; marshal of processions, and prosecutor of offenders against morality and obligations of the Rite.

Warder, Keeper of the portals; conservator of the safety of the Constellation from intrusion; examiner and voucher of all visitors, and steward at the festivals.

Sec. 8. Vacancies among the Pillars are filled as follows: The remaining Pillars by unanimous vote nominate to the M. E. Grand Luminary suitable persons for the vacancies — who must be members of their own Constellation — which said nominees will supply the vacancies until the decision of the M. E. Grand Luminary is had. Should the nomination be confirmed, the newly appointed Pillars will be endorsed upon the back of the Charter of the subordinate Constellation, by Herald, and enrolled in the Books of the Supreme Constellation as full members.

THE CORRESPONDENTS OF THE RITE

Chapter V

Sec. 1. The females alluded to in Landmark VIII, styled Correspondents, are reckoned the Ornaments of the American Adoptive Rite. Their names will be inserted in the Charter by Herald.

Sec. 2. The benefits of this Rite are mainly to the female sex. For them this temple has been reared, these walls set up. They are its glory and crown; and its value consists in the spirit in which they enter it, and the grace they throw around it.

Sec. 3. In the organization of a Subordinate Constellation the Pillars choose five Correspondents to aid them in conferring the degrees, dispensing charity, visiting the sick, and seeking out the various objects of relief. The Correspondents are responsible to the Pillars alone.

Sec. 4. The specific duties of the Correspondents respectively are found in Part II, of this volume.

Sec. 5. Changes in the Board of Correspondents must be reported to the Supreme Constellation.

THE MEMBERSHIP

Chapter VI

Sec. 1. The title of female members of this Rite is Stellae; that of male members Protectors.

Sec. 2. The lawful recipients of the American Adoptive Rite are such worthy females — being wives, widows, daughters or sisters of worthy affiliated Master Masons — as may be nominated by two or more Correspondents and unanimously elected by the Pillars of a Subordinate Constellation. If unmarried, they must have attained the age of eighteen years to be eligible.

Likewise, such worthy Master Masons, affiliated in regular Lodges of the York Rite, as may be nominated by two or more Protectors, and unanimously elected as above.

Sec. 3. The form of a petition from a lady is as follows:

To the E. Heleon, Philomath, Verger, Herald, and Warder, of .... Constellation No. ...., of the American Adoptive Rite:

"Your petitioner, the (wife, widow, daughter, or sister) of Mr. .... solicits the light of Adoptive Masonry from your Constellation.

"She pledges her honor that if the prayer of her petition is granted she will, in all respects, conform to the legal requirements of your Constellation, and be subject to the constitutional rules and regulations of the Supreme Constellation.

"(Signed) ....

"Recommended by

....

....

"Correspondents"

Sec. 4. The form of a petition from a gentleman is as follows:

To the E. Heleon, Philomath, Verger, Herald, and Warder of .... Constellation, No. .... of the American Adoptive Rite:

Your petitioner, a Master Mason, and a member in good standing in .... Lodge, No. ...., of the Ancient York Rite, held at .... solicits the light of Adoptive Masonry from your Constellation.

"He pledges his honor as a Mason, that if the prayer of his petition is granted, he will, in all respects, conform to the legal requirements of your Constellation, and be subject to the Constitutional Rules and Regulations of the Supreme Constellation.

"(Signed) ....

"Vouched for by

....

....

"Protectors"

Sec. 5. A Stella or Protector demitted from another Constellation and wishing to affiliate again, will use the following form of petition:

To the E. Heleon, Philomath, Verger, Herald, and Warder of .... Constellation, No. .... of the American Adoptive Rite:

"The undersigned, late a member of .... Constellation, No. ...., as certified by the accompanying Signet of Withdrawal, solicits affiliation in your Constellation.

"If this petition is granted she (he) pledges her (his) honor (honor as a Mason) to conform, in all respects, to the legal requirements of your Constellation.

"(Signed) ....

"Recommended by

....

....

"Stellae (Protectors)".

The petition must be accompanied by the Signet of Withdrawal from the last Constellation in which the petitioner was affiliated.

Sec. 6. Twenty-five Stellae and as many Protectors — independent of the Pillars and Correspondents — constitute the whole membership of a Subordinate Constellation: Provided, however, that Honorary members may be made without restriction as to number. As vacancies occur upon the Membership Board, they are filled as in the case of original applications.

Sec. 7. Members of Subordinate Constellations, in good standing, desiring to change their residence, affiliate with another Constellation, or withdraw from the Order, will be entitled, upon the majority vote of the members of the Constellation, to a Signet of Withdrawal in the following form:

"We have seen his Star in the East, and are come to worship."

To the Enlightened Stellae and Protectors of the American Adoptive Rite, this Signet of Withdrawal witnesseth:

That Sister ...., whose name — ne varietur — appears in the margin of this instrument, was initiated into the light (or affiliated into membership) of the Christian Star in this Constellation, on the .... day of................., 18.........

That during her connection with us, she has, in all respects, conformed to the legal requirements of this Constellation, and the Constitutional rules and regulations of the Supreme Constellation.

That in her withdrawal she bears with her the love and esteem of the officers and members of this Constellation; and we Heleon, Philomath, Verger, Herald, and Warder of .... Constellation, No. .... of the American Adoptive Rite, holden at ...., do hereby most affectionately commend her to the kindly offices and friendship of all enlightened Stellae and Protectors wherever in the journey of human life she may be found.

(Signed)	....Heleon	
	....Philomath	
	....Verger	
(Seal)	....Herald	
	....Warder	

No Signet of Withdrawal is valid without the seal of the Subordinate Constellation. For traveling purposes, the seal and signature of the Grand Secretary of the Supreme Constellation are likewise requisite.

Sec. 8. The membership of a Protector is forfeited: 1. By absence from the sessions of the Constellation for twelve consecutive months. 2. By demitting from the Masonic Lodge in which he is affiliated. 3. By suspension or expulsion from said Lodge. 4. By suspension or expulsion from the Constellation; Provided, however, that honorary members of either sex do not incur this forfeiture on account of absence from the Constellation, neither shall absence on account of protracted journeying or ill health involve any penalty.

A majority vote of members present at any stated meeting of

the Constellation may remove the forfeiture, if for the first cause. Affiliating with a Lodge will remove it for the second cause; restoration to good standing in the Lodge for the third — and in the Constellation for the fourth.

Sec. 9. The membership of a Stella is forfeited: 1. By absence from the sessions of the Constellation for twelve consecutive months. 2. By suspension or expulsion from the Constellation. 3. By the demittal, suspension or expulsion of the individual or the person through whom she was adopted upon her original petition. Provided that, if she can prove adoption through another Master Mason, affiliated and in good standing, the Pillars of the Constellation are at liberty to substitute his name on the Membership Board for the one originally entered there.

Sec. 10. The membership of a Subordinate Constellation have original powers in the following particulars:

1. In all matters of discipline involving inquiry into misconduct, and trial, and punishment for the same. Provided, however, that in all cases an appeal to the Supreme Constellation shall be allowed. Provided further that the Correspondents shall only be responsible to the Pillars and they to the Supreme Constellation.

II. In all appropriations of the funds of the Constellation.

Sec. 11. The specific duties of the members of this Order are minutely defined in their own By-Laws; in the covenant of the American Adoptive Rite, and in the Lectures attached to the five degrees, respectively. They are in general to cultivate peace and harmony towards one another; to extend relief liberally; to counsel kindly; and to extend the religion of a crucified Savior by precept and example, as opportunity may offer.

PART II — THE RITUAL

OPENING OF CONSTELLATION

Chapter I

Sec. 1. The business of the Constellation is to act upon petitions; to initiate; to dispense charity and sympathy; to confer the Five Degrees of the American Adoptive Rite and communicate the lectures of the same; to exercise discipline; likewise to take all proper measures for cultivating peace and harmony, and extending the Christian principles of morality and love among the members. Finally to aid in the important work of extending the benefits of the American Adoptive Rite to every community where there are persons entitled to receive it.

Sec. 2. The meetings of a Constellation are STATED and CALLED.

The STATED meetings are those enjoined by the By-Laws, and may be held either Weekly, or Semi-monthly, Monthly, Bi-monthly or Quarterly, at the choice of the members expressed in the By-Laws.

The CALLED meetings are those summoned at the will of Heleon, or, in his absence, by the highest Pillar in rank, upon any emergency apparent to him.

All business proper for a STATED meeting is legitimate for a CALLED meeting except the appropriation of the funds of the Constellation.

No meeting, either STATED or CALLED, is lawfully held unless the Charter is present and visible to the members and visitors.

None can be present at the opening of the Constellation save those who have received all the Degrees of the Order.

Sec. 3. The place of meeting may be a hall, private apartment, or the forest and plain. It must be sufficiently secluded to secure secrecy; and central to accommodate the members of the Constellation. Caution is essential in the selection of the place of meeting, so as to avoid slanderous imputations from the unenlightened.

A contiguous apartment for the examination of visitors &c., will be found convenient and is recommended.

Sec. 4. The paraphernalia essential to the meetings of the Constellation are one or more Bibles, Membership Board, Charter and By-Laws. To these should be added, when convenient, the Banner of the Constellation, a sword, two spring bells, and other appliances for work and instruction.

If initiation is to be performed or Degrees conferred, a Scepter, Sheaf of Grain, Crown, Cup of Wine, Loaf, Black Veil, Basket, Pitcher, Cross, and other paraphernalia will be convenient.

Every meeting, whether STATED or CALLED, should be concluded, when practicable, with a social repast.

Sec. 5. A meeting of the Constellation for any business save initiation or conferring Degrees, may be opened and held by the Pillars or a majority (three) of them.

But the number essential to initiate or confer the Degrees is five of each sex, including the Warder.

Sec. 6. Those precautionary measures which form so prominent a feature in all secret affiliated systems, whereby they are enable to detect imposters and reject them from their assemblies, are of the highest possible importance in the American Adoptive Rite, in view of the peculiar intimacy between the sexes which constitutes the prime feature and aim of this society. This intimacy is, in itself, calculated to furnish the world with a subject for slanderous imputations; and it will infallibly render any negligence allowed, though apparently slight and unimportant, serious in its consequences.

The Pillars of the Constellation are, therefore, enjoined by every principle of prudence and self-preservation, to study critically the standard measures of precaution; to exercise extraordinary vigilance in purging their assemblies; and to allow neither fear nor favor to bias them in the admission of unworthy or unenlightened visitors.

Not only will the honor of the Order suffer by any relaxation in these particulars, but wounds, not easily healed, may be inflicted upon the peace and happiness of those amiable ladies who honor us with their association.

Sec. 7. The hour for opening the Constellation having arrived — whether STATED or CALLED MEETING, the formula is the same — the Pillars will assemble in private and appoint members pro tem. to fill any vacancies both in their own number and in the number of Correspondents. This being done, they will invite the Correspondents to assist them in purging the membership board. The object of performing this ceremony at every meeting or session of the Constellation is to secure the integrity of the Society. If any are recorded upon the Membership Board who should be excluded, either on account of their own unworthiness or that of the Masons through whom they were respectively adopted, (as by suspension, expulsion, or demitting from the Lodge) their names must be obliterated by Herald and they denied admission by Warder until regularly re-instated. (See Part I, Chapt. VI, Secs. 8 and 9.)

Sec. 8.   The place of meeting must now be cleared of all persons save the Pillars and Correspondents.

Heleon addresses the Warder: Sir and Pillar! the Constellation is about to be opened for the purposes contemplated in this Charter.   (He removes it from its case, opens and displays it.) Your duties will require you to remain without, guarding, with all diligence, the entrance to this place and suffering neither fear nor favor to influence you in admitting improper visitors.   Will you perform this trust in truth and vigilance?

Warder — What guarantee have I that, in my absence, the work of the Constellation will be performed agreeably to the Constitution of the Supreme Constellation and the usages of the American Adoptive Rite?

Heleon — The honor of a Mason.

Warder — It is well — I accept it — and, if you will furnish me with the means of security, I will guard you in truth and vigilance while here assembled.

Heleon — receive this key.   (He presents him with the key of the room whereupon Warder retires to the Ante-room, locks the door on the outside, and thenceforth, until the close of the meeting, the security of the Constellation is under his sole and peculiar charge.)

Sec. 9.   Heleon — Ladies and Sirs: The hour of meeting has arrived.   The precautionary measures of security, both within and without, have been duly taken, and it is now my will that the Christian Star be formed for the purposes of improvement and Social pleasure.

Heleon takes his seat at a point opposite the door and about two paces from the wall behind him.   A small round table is placed before him at a distance of about one half the breadth of the room.   The Bible is laid upon it.   (See Diagram, Fig. 11.) A cord is then stretched from his seat to the center of the table, and a circle made with that length of cord so as to ascertain with exactness the stations of the other four Pillars.   The five, when seated, represent five points of a Star, the Bible being the center. (See Diagram, Figs. 1, 2, 3, 4, and 5.)

The stations of the Correspondents are exactly ascertained as

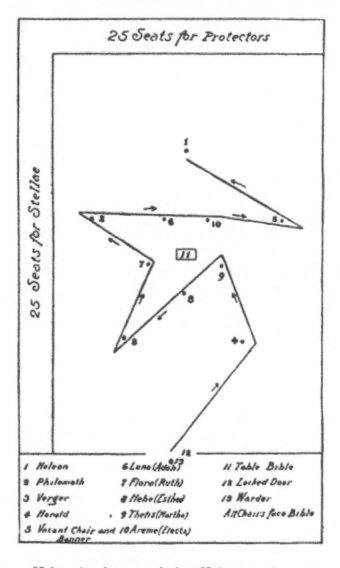

1 Heleon	*6 Luna (Adah)*	*11 Table Bible*
2 Philomath	*7 Flora (Ruth)*	*12 Locked Door*
3 Verger	*8 Hebe (Esther)*	*13 Warder*
4 Herald	*9 Thetis (Martha)*	*All Chairs face Bible*
5 Vacant Chair and Banner	*10 Areme (Electa)*	

follows: Hebe takes her seat facing Heleon on the opposite side of the Bible and at half his distance from it. The cord is now stretched from her seat to the center of the table and a circle made with that length of cord. Around that circle their seats are placed, so that, when seated, they represent five points of a Star contained within the former one and having the same center. (See Diagram, Figs. 6, 7, 8, 9, and 10.)

Full Description of Diagram

1. Station of Heleon.
2. "   " Philomath.
3. "   " Verger.
4. "   " Herald.
5. Vacant Places of the Banner.
6. Station of Luna.
7. "   " Flora.

8. Station of Hebe.
9. "   " Thetis.
10. "   " Areme.
11. Table. Bible.
12. Closed Door.
13. 25 seats for Stellae.
14. 25 "   " Protectors.

The angular line is the Labyrinth.

The Bible is opened at Isaiah LXIII.

The Banner is set up so as to exhibit the head of the Lion.

The Pillars and Correspondents should sit so as to face the Bible.

Sec. 10. The following system of Signals, peculiar to the American Adoptive Rite, is applicable to all of the work and instruction of the Order. These sounds may be made with the palms of the hands, but are best performed with spring bells in the hands of Heleon and Warder. The Stellae and Protectors should be made very familiar with them.

Signal No. I.   I—I—I—I—I   Be seated and keep silent.
"   " II.   II—I—I—I   Rise to your feet.
"   " III.   III—I—I   The Christian Star is formed. The Constellation is ready for members and visitors.
"   " IV.   IIII—I   An applicant for the light of Adoption is without.
"   " V.   IIIII   Herald will retire; inquire as to her qualifications; if found worthy, instruct her and conduct her in.
"   " VI.   I—IIII   A sister partially enlightened is without and craves further light in Adoption.

18

"	"	VII. I—I—III	The Correspondents will retire; greet your sister with an Adoptive welcome; instruct her and conduct her in.
"	"	VIII. I—II—II	The Constellation is about to be closed.
"	"	IX. Confusedly five raps.	The Constellation is closed. Open the door.

In making these signals pause the space of one second between each set of sounds. Where sounds are marked as coming together, make them as rapidly as possible, only taking care to make them distinct from each other, so that they can readily be counted.

Sec. 11. The Christian Star having been formed, (see Sec. 9th) Heleon makes Signal No. 1.

Warder responds by the same signal from without, and prepares to admit members and visitors.

Members are admitted by displaying the Tessera, but as Warder is legally responsible for the security of the Constellation while open, he will be expected to satisfy himself thoroughly as to the qualifications of visitors, before admission. The communication of the semi-annual memorial; the avouchal of one or more members who are personally conversant with the visitor's qualifications as member of the Adoptive Rite in good standing; the Tessera; and an examination upon all the Signs, Passes, and means of recognition of the Rite, form the various safeguards at the command of Warder — to be used more or less rigidly, at his discretion. The evil that would result from the admission of an imposter is sufficiently obvious to impress him with the vital importance of his position.

See Sec. 14 of this Chapter of a description of the Tessera.

See Sec. 15 of this Chapter for the manner of communicating the semi-annual Memorial.

See Sec. 16 of this Chapter for further instructions in relation to examining visitors.

Sec. 12. The door is opened by Warder for the admission of only two persons at a time. When convenient, they should be one of each sex — the lady walking on the right.

They pass the LABYRINTH according to the instructions in

Section 17 of this Chapter. The lady should take the left of the gentleman when they pass Philomath.

As each chair is passed they make the Initiation Sign — See Section 18 of this Chapter — and receive from its occupant the Responsive Sign. See Sec. 19 of this Chapter. Chair No. 5 being vacant, the signs are omitted in passing that place.

Arriving before Heleon, each presents a Tessera to that official, who examines it, and if found correct, invites them to proper seats. See Diagram, for full instructions as to seats of officers, members, and visitors, and the general arrangement of a Constellation when opened.

Sec. 13. The members and visitors having entered, the ceremony of opening the Constellation is thus performed:

Heleon, addressing Philomath — Sir and Pillar: Will you communicate to us some of that Divine Light which is appropriated to the interesting work in which we are about to engage?

Philomath — What guarantee have I that we are secure from spies, traitors, and imposters?

Heleon — The honor of a Mason.

Philomath — It is well; I accept it.

He advances to the Bible, faces Heleon and reads aloud the first six verses of Isaiah LXIII.

Heleon — It is well. The Prophet has spoken eloquently of Him who was yet to come. But communicate to us Light from the same Divine source, in proof that Jesus Christ was that Mighty to Save, of whom the Prophet spoke.

Philomath reads the last five verses of I Peter 11 (21st-25th).

Heleon — It is well.

He strikes Signal No. 2.

Let us pray: — Holy and Merciful God! who hath revealed thyself to us in the person of thy Son Jesus Christ, that they who believe on Him might not perish, but have everlasting life! grant to each of us here assembled a saving knowledge of Him, — that in His merits our sins may be forgiven; in His strength our weakness may be lost; and in the triumph of His resurrection, our death may be swallowed up in victory. May the light of thy Divine Truth illumine us as we contemplate Him in His various relations to mankind, as the WORD, the LILY of the Valley, the

20

SUN of Righetousness, the LAMB of God, and the LION of the Tribe of Judah! And may the instructive lessons we here enjoy work due effect in our hearts and actions, here and elsewhere, now and forever. Amen.

He strikes Signal No. 1.

Here commences the opening Lecture given under the instructions of Philomath.

Philomath — Let us attend to the instructive lessons of our Order.

We have five Degrees named respectively, JEPHTHAH'S DAUGHTER, RUTH, ESTHER, MARTHA, and ELECTA. In these, we contemplate certain exalted virtues in their relationship to this history of our Lord Jesus Christ, that perfect Exemplar of all virtue.

In His eventful and blessed life we view Him resigning His life to fulfill His Father's oath that the soul that sinneth shall die; forsaking His princely mansion in heaven to dwell in a humble place on earth; offering Himself a victim to rescue His people from impending and eternal death; relying, with unswerving faith, upon the promises of God; and, finally, sacrificing all things, fame, power, friends, and life, in testimony of the religion He came to establish. Was there ever Love like His?

The lessons of our Order teach, in emblematic guise, these grand truths. Sisters, rehearse your respective portions of them.

Sister Luna, whose history have you? (As each Correspondent replies to her respective questions, she rises and makes the initiation sign.)

Luna — That of Adah, the daughter of Jephthah the Gileadite.

Philomath — What was her lot?

Luna — To resign her life in fulfilment of the oath of her father — even as Christ the Word of God resigned his.

Philomath — Have you an emblem?

Luna — I have THE SWORD which, in the hands of her own father, became the instrument of her death.

Philomath — Have you a sign?

Luna — I have this: (She gives the hailing sign of Jephthah's Daughter as described in Sec. 20 of this Chapter.)

Philomath — What are its allusions?

Luna — It alludes to the Firmness with which Adah adhered to

21

her determination to die in the light, suffering no stain to rest upon her memory after death.

Philomath — What symbolic lessons have you?

Luna — My color BLUE, — which is the hue of distant mountains under Judah's clear sky, — reminds me of the two months' stay made by Adah in the mountains, while fortifying her mind against the terrors of a violent death.

Philomath — It is well; and when a Sister in distress hails us with that sign, we will recall the merits of Jephthah's Daughter, and of you, my sister, her representative; be reminded of our Covenant of Adoption; and, responding with the PASS of this Degree, afford her prompt relief. Brothers, shall it be so?

All reply, "Even so!"

Sister Flora, whose history have you?

Flora — That of Ruth the Moabitess, the widow of Mahlon of Bethlehem.

Philomath — What was her lot?

Flora — To forsake her native country, princely friends, and a beloved home, for the love of God, — even as CHRIST, THE LILY of the Valley, forsook His.

Philomath — Have you an emblem?

Flora — I have — THE SHEAF — which, in the field of Boaz, became the means of preserving her life and exhibiting the benevolence of a faithful Brother.

Philomath — Have you a sign?

Flora — I have this: (She gives the hailing sign of Ruth, as described in Sec. 20 of this Chapter.)

Philomath — What are its allusions?

Flora — It alludes to the faith in God which, in her hour of hunger, loneliness and despair, buoyed her up to declare, by this expressive sign, her innocence of wrong and her trust in Heaven.

Philomath — What symbolic lessons have you?

Flora — My Color YELLOW, — which is the hue of the barley fields on the plains of Judah, — reminds me that, in that place of harvest, all her prayers were answered, her faith rewarded, and her trust in God vindicated.

Philomath — It is well; and when a sister in distress hails us with that sign, we will recall the merits of RUTH and of you, my sister, her representative; be reminded of our Covenant of Adoption, and, responding with the PASS of this Degree, afford her prompt relief. Brothers, shall it be so?

All reply, "Even so."

Sister Hebe, whose history have you?

Hebe — That of Esther, the Queen of Persia, one of the despised people of God, exiles in a cruel land.

Philomath — What was her lot?

Hebe — To offer her crown and life to rescue her people from impending death — even as CHRIST, THE SUN of Righteousness, offered His.

Philomath — Have you an emblem?

Hebe — I have — the CROWN — which, denoting royalty, is the measure of that vast sacrifice so cheerfully made by Esther for the preservation of her people.

Philomath — Have you a sign?

Hebe — I have this: (She gives the hailing sign of Esther, as described in Sec. 20 of this Chapter.)

Philomath — What are its allusions?

Hebe — It alludes to the Pledge made her by the King, her husband, in acknowledgment of her talents and virtue.

Philomath — What symbolic lessons have you?

Hebe — My Color WHITE, which is the hue of the silken robes of ESTHER — reminds me that, in the spotless purity of Christ alone I can expect to find favor at the Throne of God.

Philomath — It is well; and when a sister in distress hails us with that sign we will recall the merits of ESTHER, and of you, my sister, her representative; be reminded of our Covenant of Adoption, and, responding with the PASS of this Degree, afford her prompt relief. Brothers, shall it be so?

All reply, "Even so!"

Sister Thetis, whose history have you?

Thetis — That of Martha of Bethany, sister of Lazarus whom Jesus loved.

Philomath — What was her lot?

Thetis — To mourn desolate, four weary days and nights, the loss of friends, even as CHRIST THE LAMB of God, mourned His.

Philomath — Have you an emblem?

Thetis — I have; the PILLAR RENT, which denotes the sudden death of Lazarus.

Philomath — Have you a sign?

Thetis — I have this: (She gives the hailing sign of Martha as described in Sec. 20 of this Chapter.)

Philomath — What are its allusions?

Thetis — It alludes to that appealing glance which Martha, in the depths of her misery, cast into the countenance of her friend and Saviour.

Philomath — What symbolic lessons have you?

Thetis — My Color GREEN, which is the hue of spring, and covers every grave as a mantle, reminds me that as Lazarus came forth at the breath of the Lord Jesus Christ, so shall I, in the springtime of the Resurrection, be summoned from my grave by the same commanding voice.

Philomath — It is well; and when a sister in distress hails us with that sign, we will recall the merits of Martha, and of you, my sister, her representative; be reminded of our Covenant of Adoption, and, responding with the PASS of this Degree, afford her prompt relief. Brothers, shall it be so?

All reply, "Even so."

Philomath — Sister Areme, whose history have you?

Areme — That of Electa, the martyr of Christ; the wife of the Past Grand Master of Masons.

Philomath — What was her lot?

Areme — To resign her life for a testimony to the power and importance of religion, even as CHRIST, THE LION of the Tribe of Judah, resigned his.

Philomath — Have you an emblem?

Areme — I have the JOINED HANDS, which denoting ardent hospitality, teaches that, though the Christian Saint could not render to God the benefits received from Him, she neglected no opportunity to dispense charity to His people.

Philomath — Have you a sign?

Areme — I have this: (She gives the hailing sign of Electa, as described in Sec. 20 of this Chapter.)

Philomath — What are its allusions?

Areme — It alludes to the CROSS upon which Electa found a passage from this cruel world to a home of eternal rest.

24

Philomath — What symbolic lessons have you?

Areme — My color RED, which is the hue of blood and wine, reminds me to dispense of my temporal means to the poor, even as the Redeemer gave His heart's best blood to save me from eternal death.

Philomath — It is well. And when a sister in distress hails us with that sign, we will recall the merits of Electa and of you, my sister, her representative; be reminded of our Covenant of Adoption, and responding with the PASS of this Degree, afford her prompt relief. Brothers, shall it be so?

All reply, "Even so."

Enlightened Heleon! the Lecture is closed. Our Sisters are found to be well versed in the lessons of the Order.

Here, if convenient, the Constellation may be called up to sing an opening Ode appropriate to the work.

Heleon — I declare this Constellation prepared for the diffusion of light.

He gives signal No. 1, and the Constellation is considered to be open.

It is urgently recommended to the ladies who officiate as Correspondents in this Constellation, that each one commit to memory at least her own six responses in the opening ceremonies. They contain the spirit of the whole Rite; the lessons they convey are transcendently beautiful; the effect of the dialogue is vastly enhanced by each portion being uttered as if extemporaneously; and, in short, the intention of this Rite will only be partially subserved if the passages from the Hue Books are merely read by the officers instead of being spoken.

At the first organization of the Constellation, or in the event of a difficulty in finding ladies disposed to take this trouble, the parts may be delivered by gentlemen; but the result will not be so pleasing as when the Correspondents do it in the manner prescribed.

Sec. 14. The Tessera is a metallic object in the form of a Five-pointed Star, the points being so disposed that one is directed downwards, on the front of which appears the Lion, the symbol of this Order, — on the back the name of the Stella (or Protector) who presents it, and the name and number of Constellation of which she (or he) is or was last a Member. The theory of the

American Adoptive Rite is that every Stella and Protector is provided with a Tessera, to answer as a visible token of membership in traveling and to present to Warder at the door of the Constellation as a testimonial of qualifications.

In such cases, however, as the loss of the Tessera, or its being absent, or the party not having provided herself (or himself) with one, Warder will provide in its stead a slip of card, or paper containing the name, locality, &c. of the party; and this may be exhibited to Heleon on entering, as a substitute.

No person, member or visitor, can, under any circumstances, enter a Constellation without exhibiting the Tessera or its substitute to Warder and Heleon.

Sec. 15. The Semi-annual Memorial, see Part I, Chap. 3, Sec. 2, is a means of communication chiefly designed for traveling purposes.

It originated with the M. E. Grand Luminary, and is communicated by the Grand Secretary through Herald of each Constellation to each of the Pillars and Correspondents thereof; — likewise to such of the Stellae and Protectors as may contemplate a journey.

But, as no visitor can be admitted into a Constellation without giving this as one of the proofs of qualification, it is advised that, where there are two or more Constellations in the same place or vicinity, the Memorial be communicated to all the members of both, for the furtherance of social pleasures and the general prosperity of the Order. And either of the Pillars is authorized to communicate it, at discretion, to any of the Stellae or Protectors of his own Constellation.

The manner of its communication is as follows: — the Pillar about to give it, collects four members together, who are entitled to receive it, and disposes of the third portion of it first. This is followed up by the first portion — then the fifth and fourth, — he reserving the second to himself. Having thus communicated it, it is passed around the circle sufficiently often to impress it upon the memory of each, and a lecture is given to the effect that they are not entitled to communicate it to any one; that they cannot enter a Constellation as visitors unless they are in possession of it; that it is changed and becomes inoperative after the first day of the succeeding January or July, as the case may be; that it is illegal to write it for the better recollection of it; and that a visitor on being examined must give the third, first and fifth portions in the order mentioned, and these only.

A person demitting from a Constellation is not entitled to receive the Semi-annual Memorial. This injunction of course debars such an one from visiting any Constellation save his (or her) own after the next semi-annual change of Memorial.

Sec. 16. The examination of visitors who are not otherwise vouched for, devolves upon the Warder, who alone is responsible for their qualifications. A legal avouchal is the declaration of some members of his own Constellation, or of a person whom he knows to be a member of some other Constellation, that he (or she) knows the visitor to be a member of a Constellation in good standing. But even in that case the applicant must be in possession of the Memorial or be denied admittance.

When the communication of the Memorial is demanded from a visitor, Warder will require him (or her) to give the third, first and fifth portions, he giving the second and fourth only. (Sec. 11 of this Chapter.)

Sec. 17. The Guide to the Labyrinth is given in Manuscript; (see Tuilleur).

Sec. 18. The description of the Initiation Sign is given in Manuscript (see Tuilleur). It represents the manner of grasping the Scriptures while receiving the Covenant of Adoption.

Sec. 19. The description of the Responsive Sign is given in Manuscript (see Tuilleur). It points out the source from whence Adoptive Masonry receives its illumination.

Sec. 20. The Signs of each Degree are explained in manuscript (see Tuilleur). They are suggestive of the actions upon which the Degrees respectively are founded, and should be well understood by every votary of Adoptive Masonry. In the hour of peril they form the means of relief and escape to the otherwise helpless lady, — and who can know what day or what hour that time may come? They are the manner of claim upon the honor and chivalry of the Brother, — and who can know what day or what hour that claim may be made? Let each Stella, then, for her own security, and each Protector, for his own honor, impress these signs deeply upon the tablets of memory, that they may

27

never be overlooked or disregarded, when the time comes to use them.

The Hailing Sign of JEPHTHAH'S DAUGHTER represents her unveiling three separate times, despite her father's commands; and, finally, her vigorous refusal to submit to the proffered indignity.

The Hailing Sign of RUTH represents her silent declaration of innocence and devout appeal to God.

The Hailing Sign of ESTHER represents her appeal to her husband's long-remembered vow, and the manner of his recognition of the sign, and assent to her wishes.

The Hailing Sign of MARTHA represents her earnest glance, from her place at Christ's feet into his benignant countenance.

The Hailing Sign of ELECTA represents the manner of her death.

Sec. 21.   The Constellation is closed as follows: — When the work which was presented for the purpose is performed, or the fitting hour for closing has arrived, the minutes of the meeting are read for correction.

Heleon then makes Signal No. 8, and then Signal No. 2.   The following prayer is then offered:

"Holy and Merciful God!   Thou who answereth prayer and doth not scorn the petition of the humblest of thy children — bestow upon us, in our parting, that spirit of affection which can resist the selfishness and coldness of the world, and cause us to remember our Covenant with one another, and with Thee.   Preserve us, Oh! Mighty Lord, from the accidents of life and the sting of death; and grant that, in due time, all of us may be permitted, with loving hearts, to assemble again under these pleasing bonds for our own instruction, for thine honor, and for the good of our fellow men.   We ask through Christ our Saviour.   Amen."

A closing Ode, appropriate to the work, may be sung.

Any of the prayers recorded in this volume may be omitted at pleasure and others improvised in their stead.

Heleon then pronounces the Constellation closed, and makes Signal No. 9, to that effect.

THE INITIATION

Chapter II

Sec. 1. The ceremonial of Initiation into the American Adoptive Rite is not reckoned a Degree, but rather a mental preparation and a trial of the temper and a spirit of the applicant, preparatory to her being favored with the full light of Adoption. One month's time must be given between the Initiation and the Degrees, save where Dispensations are granted by the officers of the Supreme Constellation, permitting a more rapid advancement.

The system of Initiation comprises the whole of the Covenant of Adoption, which must be carefully explained to the applicant before requiring her to receive it.

It is requisite, in general, if the candidate is a lady, that she have one or two of her female friends with her, members of the Order, to bear her company in the ante-room, until she enters the Constellation. But the presence of her husband, father or brother may be substituted in case the membership of the Constellation is too small to spare the ladies from the room.

For form of petition, see Part I, Chap. 6, Sec. 3.

Sec. 2. In considering a petition for the light of Adoptive Masonry, let these five points of inquiry be made:

I. Is the petition in due form, signed by the applicant's own hand, recommended by the Constitutional number, and accompanied by the fee required by the By-Laws? — The duty of answering this inquiry devolves upon Herald.

II. Is the applicant a suitable subject for the American Adoptive Rite — if a lady, 18 years of age and upwards, the wife, widow, daughter, or sister of an affiliated Master Mason in good standing? — if a gentleman, an affiliated Master Mason in good standing. The duty of answering this inquiry rests with Verger.

III. Is the applicant personally acceptable to every officer and member of the Constellation so far as can be known? — The duty of answering this rests with Warder.

IV. Is there a vacancy upon the Membership Board? — The duty of answering this inquiry, as well as the first, rests with Herald.

V.   Is the applicant of sound mind and capable of acquiring a knowledge of the Rite? — The duty of answering this inquiry rests with Philomath.

Sec. 3.   The petition, duly signed and recommended, is considered in private by the Pillars of the Constellation who have the sole right to select the material for the work of Adoptive Masonry. They are at liberty, however, to ask advice from the Correspondents and other members, and even when they think proper, to admit them to ballot; but the Pillars alone will be held responsible to the Supreme Constellation for the character of the initiates and the correctness of the work.   For while we grant the impolicy of admitting a new member who is offensive to any of the old members, and advise that such a step should in general be avoided, yet the Supreme Constellation will not authorize any deviation from the Landmark that "the sole responsibility of the work is in the Pillars, who form the only legal communication between the Supreme and the Subordinate Constellation."

Sec. 4.   The petition having been thus thoroughly considered, the vote must be taken by secret ballot and the result recorded by Herald.   But as it is legal for either of the Pillars to object to further advancement at any time previous to the applicant taking the Fifth Degree, her name must not be recorded on the Membership Board until that consummation.

If the ballot is favorable the petitioner may at once be initiated. If not, an interval of at least three months must elapse before the application can be renewed.

Sec. 5.   The applicant, if a lady, being elected, and in waiting, a communication to that effect is made by Warder by means of Signal No. 4.   In reply Heleon makes Signal No. 5.   Herald then retires to the ante-room, with the petition in his hand, introduces himself to the candidate as an official member of the Constellation and thus addresses her:

Herald — Are you the lady whose name is appended to this petition?

Applicant — I am.

Herald — Do you still entertain the desire expressed in this petition to receive the light of Adoptive Masonry?

Applicant — I do.

Herald — Who will be responsible to the Constellation for the good faith of this lady?

Warder — By my knowledge of the Masonic Brethren who have recommended her petition, I will.

Herald — It is well — I accept it.

It behooves me then as one of the Pillars of this Constellation to instruct you in the general nature of the Covenant of Adoption and explain to you the first and second portions of it . This Covenant is the solemn pledge or promise which you must make before you can be admitted into our Order. But we do not wish you to make it, nor would we permit you to make it, save with your own consent and with a full understanding of what is implied by it. Listen to me, then — and after I am done, should you be unwilling to bind yourself thus solemnly, you may, without impediment or offense, retire from this place.

The objects for which we are banded together, are to comfort, protect and aid each other through the Labyrinth of human life, and make its hardships light by means of cheerful companionship, and social pleasures. We are willing you should join us in this pleasing work.

We are in possession of certain signs, passes, ceremonies, and lectures, by means of which we recognize each other wherever we go. We are willing to make you acquainted with these secrets, that you, too, may be recognized as an Adopted Mason.

We are governed by a Supreme Constellation which makes our laws and regulations uniform with those of all other members of this Order throughout America, and by a form of By-Laws framed by ourselves. We are bound to obey these Rules, Regulations and By-Laws so long as we remain members of the Society. In this obedience we shall expect you to share.

We are tonguetied against slandering any member of this Order; and bound with chains and fetters against doing one of them any manner of wrong. You will in like manner be placed under restraint.

We are all of us in faith, Christians; and it is a large part of the business of this Society to rehearse the life and doctrines of

Christ, and endeavor to imitate and practice upon his example. In this faith, and in these works, you, too, will be expected to participate.

Is there any thing thus far explained to you that you would not be willing to promise?

Applicant — There is not.

Herald — Do you, then, covenant your honor, as a woman, and your truth, as a believer in the Bible, that you will never reveal our secrets and that you will be obedient to the Rules, Regulations and By-Laws of our Society?

Applicant — I do.

Herald — It is well. Warder, give us admittance to the Constellation!

Herald enters with the applicant and the door is closed. Herald takes his seat, as Thetis comes forward, takes the Applicant by both hands and thus addresses her:

Thetis — Welcome, my dear friend, to our Constellation. The recommendations you bring us have convinced us that you are a proper subject for the light of Adoptive Masonry. We trust that the lessons we shall teach you here, will both please and instruct you. Human life is a Labyrinth through which we, wander, too often, alas! blindly and in ignorance. It is good for us to have a friendly form by our side who has trod this way before us, and a friendly hand that can guide us with infallible certainty and safety through its most intricate mazes. Such a companion may be found in Jesus Christ; who lived as WE are living, died as WE must die, and went before us to heaven to prepare a place for us.

Permit me, however, on the present occasion, to act as your guide through a Labyrinth which otherwise you could not pass, and to lead you to the presence of our enlightened chief officer. But receive, first of all, this copy of the Divine Guide of Life. Hands her a small Bible and teaches her how to grasp it as described in Chap 1, Sec. 18.

The LABYRINTH is now passed as described in Chap. 1, Sec. 17.

As they pass the station of Herald (see Diagram) they are accosted:

Herald — What bringest thou?

Thetis — I know not.

Herald — You know not?

Thetis — But I have a hope.

Herald — What hopest thou, then?

Thetis — Affection.

Herald — It is well. Pass, Affection!

As they pass the station of Thetis, they halt:

Thetis — This is the seat which I have vacated for a time, that I may assist your wandering steps through our Labyrinth. We are taught in the lessons of Adoptive Masonry to resign, at times, our comforts and ease, that by so doing, we can benefit our fellow creatures. Be seated.

The applicant takes the vacant chair.

Soon may you be enlightened, my dear friend, to fill this or some other station in our Order. Whenever wearied on the journey of human life, may you always find, as you do now, a friend, who has a place and a heart to refresh you. Rise, now, and let us be going.

The candidate rises and the Labyrinth is resumed. As they pass the station of Hebe they are accosted:

Hebe — What bringest thou?

Thetis — I know not.

Hebe — You know not?

Thetis — But I have a hope.

Hebe — What hopest thou, then?

Thetis — Amiability.

Hebe — It is well. Pass, Amiability.

As they pass the station of Verger, they are accosted:

Verger — What bringest thou?

Thetis — I know not.

Verger — You know not?

Thetis — But I have a hope.

Verger — What hopest thou, then?

Thetis — Charity.

Verger — It is well. It behooves me now, as one of the Pillars of this Constellation to instruct you in the third and fourth Sections of the Covenant of Adoption.

The Society of Adoptive Masonry is bound together by ties of mutual aid and relief. We counsel each other when in difficulty;

sympathize with each other when in affliction; and give aid to each other when in distress. Are you willing to covenant your honor, as a woman, and your truth, as a believer in the Bible, that you will take a zealous part with us in this work?

Applicant — I am.

Verger — It is well. Adoptive Masons, deriving their knowledge from the pages of the Blessed Volume you bear, have learned that we are exposed through every moment of our lives to be led away by temptations. We pray that we may not be led into temptation. We encourage each other to resist temptation, and we are solemnly pledged not to do an injury to one another, by word or act. Are you willing to covenant your honor, as a woman, and your truth, as a believer in the Bible, that you will take a zealous part with us in this work?

Applicant — I am.

Verger — It is well. Pass, Charity!

As they pass the station of Flora, they are accosted:

Flora — What bringest thou?

Thetis — I know not!

Flora — You know not?

Thetis — But I have a hope.

Flora — What hopest thou, then?

Thetis — Constancy.

Flora — It is well. Pass, Constancy.

As they pass the station of Philomath they are accosted:

Philomath — What bringest thou?

Thetis — I know not!

Philomath — You know not?

Thetis — But I have a hope.

Philomath — What hopest thou, then?

Thetis — Delicacy.

Philomath — It is well. It behooves me now, as one of the Pillars of this Constellation, to instruct you in the fifth and last Section of the Covenant of Adoption.

The Society of Adoptive Masonry is a Society of Christians. None enter our ranks save those who believe that Jesus Christ is the Son of God, the Redeemer of the World, and the Almighty

Saviour. We teach no lessons but such as relate to Him. We make no prayers but through His holy name. We entertain no religious hopes but those which are founded upon His Birth, Life, Death, Resurrection and Ascension. Are you willing to covenant your honor, as a woman, and your truth, as a believer in the Bible, that you will take a zealous part with us in the work of promulgating these truths?

Applicant — I am.

Philomath — It is well. Pass, Delicacy.

As they pass the station of Luna, they are accosted:

Luna — What bringest thou?

Thetis — I know not.

Luna — You know not?

Thetis — But I have a hope.

Luna — What hopest thou, then?

Thetis — Discretion.

Luna — It is well. Pass, Discretion.

As they pass the station of Areme, they are accosted:

Areme — What bringest thou?

Thetis — I know not.

Areme — You know not?

Thetis — But I have a hope.

Areme — What hopest thou, then?

Thetis — Faith.

Areme — It is well. Pass, Faith.

As they pass the station of the Banner they halt:

Thetis — This is the second period of your rest. Be seated.

The Applicant takes the vacant chair.

You are now very near the end of your Labyrinth, and so are you not far from the end of human life. Above you is suspended the Banner of our Order, the Lion of the Tribe of Judah. Under the shadow of this Rock may you dwell. And when, in the last stages of the Labyrinth of life, old age shall admonish you of your speedy end, may you be revived by the unfailing strength of Him whom you have faithfully served. Rise, let us be going.

They pass in front of Heleon and halt:

Heleon — What bringest thou?

Thetis — Hopes, hopes — many and bright. A field of virtues in which the principles of our Order may produce an abundant harvest.

Heleon — It is well. May they be amply realized. And that they may, it behooves me, as the chief Pillar of this Constellation to bind you, my sister, to us and to our Order by the Covenant of Adoption.

This covenant was explained to you, my sister, at various stages of your journey. You consented to receive it. Yet, even now, if you have any reluctance to make these solemn promises, we will release you from your pledge, and permit you to withdraw. I will repeat it to you, lest you may, in any manner, be deceived.

If any explanation is demanded by the Applicant, she is entitled, at this stage, to be thoroughly enlightened upon the nature of the Covenant of Adoption. It is highly solemn and binding; while it is not, strictly speaking, an oath, it is equally impressive and bears upon it every mark of earnestness and truth. We require that it be repeated, clause by clause, by Heleon, before the Applicant is permitted to give her assent to any part of it.

(For the form of the Covenant of Adoption, see Tuilleur.)

After the candidate has been made satisfied upon each clause of the Covenant and consents to take it, Heleon will place a small Bible in her hands, in the manner described in the Initiation Sign (see Tuilleur) and explain to her that the sanction of her pledge is the Word of God which she is now clasping. In that position, let her give her assent as above enjoined.

Heleon — Do you to all these pledges covenant your honor, as a woman, and your truth, as a believer in the Bible?

Applicant — I do.

Heleon — It is well. We readily accept the pledge you make to us. We share with you in this Covenant and do now accept you into our band. Herald, make record that Sister ...., the .... of Brother ...., an affiliated Master Mason, is now initiated into the American Adoptive Rite. Sisters, give her a kind assurance of her welcome among us.

The Correspondents advance and take her kindly by the hand with words of welcome and pleasure, and she is then conducted to the station of the Banner, and seated. If others are to be initiated at the same meeting, she is requested to take a place with the female members of the Constellation until the ceremonial is completed that the lecture may be given to all the Initiates at once. When the time comes for the Lecture the Initiates are seated near Heleon, who, first instructing them in the Initiation Sign, thus addresses them:

Sec. 6. Heleon — My Sisters! We hail with true pleasure your coming among us. The work of Adoptive Masonry is amply sufficient for us all, and we shall rejoice to find you excelling in your zeal that of the most devoted members of our Society.

We are laboring to increase our own happiness and to promote that of others. Our experience and the wisdom we gain from the Scriptures alike teach us that this world is a harsh, unfriendly scene, poorly adapted to impart felicity; and that it is chiefly by combining the efforts of the good and true, in the work of morality and religion, that happiness is to be acquired and extended. The greater our ability to do good, the more pleasure we shall enjoy.

We meet in private that we may arrange our plans for the good work in which we are engaged, without interruption from those who cannot understand or sympathize with us. In our meetings we strive to learn our duty as beings who possess an immortal part, and when we return home it is our care to perform it. We cultivate a spirit of harmony that the Enemy of our Souls may acquire no advantage over us.

And as a large portion of our work as Adopted Masons lies in acquiring the doctrines and temper of Jesus Christ, whom truly to know is everlasting Life, we often unite to address the Heavenly Throne and to plead with God that the very spirit of Faith and Wisdom may descend upon us and make our meeting-place a place like Heaven. In such a prayer let us now with cheerful faith combine.

He makes Signal No. 2.

"Source of all Wisdom, Truth and Love! grant to us that, in the reception of these persons, we may add strength to our strength and grace to our grace. Oh, may the golden chain thus lengthened become the brighter for these links and be strengthened for the great work we do. Enlarge our powers to benefit mankind and to honor God. And when, one by one, each link shall fall away in death, may the parting be temporary and the meeting eternal. In the world where death comes not, may we realize the full happiness of loving and serving Thee forever. We ask through Christ our Saviour, Amen." Heleon makes Signal No. 1, and thus the Initiation is closed.

The Initiation Sign and the Responsive Sign are now taught, as in Chap. 1, Secs. 18 and 19, and the plan of the Labyrinth rehearsed. Such further explanations may be given as may appear proper to the occasion, and the meeting closes with a social repast.

One month must elapse before the Initiates can receive their Degrees.

Sec. 7. In the Initiation of gentlemen the work and lectures must be varied to suit. The Labyrinth will be taught by Herald instead of Thetis, and the other portions of the ceremonial changed at discretion, or even entirely omitted.

It is not important, however, that the ceremonial be performed at all in such cases; only we enjoin that the Covenant of Adoption be given in the manner prescribed in Sec. 5 of this Chapter, and that the Signs be carefully explained to them.

Sec. 8. Nothing can be more important to the interests of the Adoptive Rite than that the initiation be performed with solemn impressiveness and that degree of earnestness that interests the feelings. With this the Initiate returns home pleased, and instructed; and when permitted to re-visit the Constellation, for the purpose of receiving the Degrees, she seizes the opportunity with eagerness, ardently anticipating further gratification.

To the end that nothing be inadequately performed, let the officers, as far as possible, memorize their respective portion, or if that is impracticable, familiarize themselves by repeated perusals of the text, that they may readily pronounce them, when the ceremony demands it.

The difficulty of realizing the dramatic effect of a dialogue by a mere perusal is very great. It must be seen to be appreciated. The machinery, the manner of the actors, the impressiveness of the ceremonial, and the mystery thrown around the whole, must be taken into consideration before this beautiful ceremonial of initiation can be properly estimated. Further, it must be recollected that its chief impressiveness is designed to affect the female mind.

JEPHTHAH'S DAUGHTER

Chapter III

Sec. 1. This Degree, together with the subsequent ones, is regularly conferred only upon females. Brethren who have been initiated into the American Adoptive Rite as in Chap. 2, Sec. 6, will acquire a knowledge of the Five Degrees by witnessing the ceremony of conferring them upon the ladies. There is no pledge or covenant in any of the Degrees additional to that contained in the initiation, but this must be repeated in each Degree.

A Sister, having been regularly Initiated as in Chapter 2, must wait at least one month before she is eligible to receive the Degrees.

But this rule may be suspended by a Dispensation from any of the officers of the Supreme Constellation, and in the organization of a new Constellation, authority is always given to the Pillars to dispense with this requisition at least to the number of five applicants.

When more than one application is made for the Degrees at the same meeting, the first person elected should be caused to pause after receiving the First Degree and required to witness the conferring it upon the others, before she advances further; the same arrangement may be adopted in relation to the other Degrees.

The whole of each Lecture should be rehearsed in immediate connection with the Degree to which it relates.

No preparation of the candidates, save a willing and obedient spirit, is demanded for this or the subsequent Degrees. But as a means of ascertaining the feelings which prompt the applicant to advance, it is recommended that she be solicited to devote a sum, small or great according to her ability and disposition, to the "Widow's Fund" of the Constellation, as the First Fruits of her Adoption. Moneys so received must be set apart in strict accordance with the wishes of the donor.

No ballot is demanded upon an application for the Degrees, and no fee shall be charged for them. Whatever ballots or fees are required by the Regulations of the Order, they must be satisfied in the action upon the original petition.

The room is prepared for the ceremonial of Degrees by dissolving the Christian Star; removing the chair and table; and dividing the apartment into two parts by means of a curtain; that portion nearest the door of entrance to comprise about two-thirds of the room, which should be well lighted throughout.

Songs and instrumental music form delightful accompaniments to each Degree, and should always be introduced when practicable.

The plan adopted in conferring the Degrees is, for some one of the Correspondents to represent the Candidate not only in the dialogue (which of course, is unavoidable), but likewise in the ceremonial. This course certainly deprives the scene of much interest to the Candidate's mind, which would be more forcibly impressed were she to perform these parts herself. But the difficulty of arranging the work for this seemed to us insuperable.

We leave the matter, however, to the discretion of the Pillars. If they can arrange it upon a plan analogical with that adopted in conferring the Degrees in Symbolic Masonry, they are authorized and recommended to do so.

It is recommended further, that great care be exercised in practicing upon the Signs and Passes, that they may be kept entirely distinct, both in name and nature. A little confusion at first will be apt to embarrass the whole of the after-work. For the better recollection of the Hailing Signs, they may be styled respectively: "The Daughter's Sign"—"The Widow's Sign"—"The Wife's Sign"—"The Sister's Sign"—"The Christian's Sign."

Sec. 2. The paraphernalia necessary for the Degree of Jephthah's Daughter are a sword, a heavy black veil, and a wreath of flowers.

Sec. 3. The Degree of Jephthah's Daughter or the Daughter's Degree comprises the history of Adah, only child of Jephthah the Gileadite, who resigned her life to fulfill the oath of her father. The Scriptural account of the transaction is contained in Judges XI, verses 35 to 40. The ancient Degree of "The Eastern Star" affords the traditions upon which the ceremonial and lectures are based.

Jephthah is represented in the dialogue by Heleon; Adah by Luna. All the members of the Constellation, male and female, should take part in the drama, to give it due effect.

Sec. 4. The Candidate being announced by Warder, in the

ante-room, as in readiness, by Signal No. 6, Heleon makes Signal No. 7 in reply; the five Correspondents then retire to the ante-room to receive her, and Luna thus addresses her:

Luna — My dear Sister! you are about to represent Adah, that devoted woman, the daughter of Jephthah, the Gileadite, who re-signed her life to fulfill the oath of her father. Carefully observe whatever passes under your notice, my dear Sister, and let the im-pressive lessons of this Degree sink deeply into your heart.

Warder repeats the Covenant of Adoption to her and demands her assent to it. The ladies then enter in company and remain by the door. Behind the curtain, a sound is heard as of the tramp-ling of feet and of music. After listening for a moment, Luna, who represents Jephthah's Daughter in this ceremony, speaks:

Luna — Hosanna! they come! they come! Oh the rapture of this hour! For this have I waited; for this my prayers have as-cended day and night to heaven. Hosanna! they come! they come! Soon I shall meet my father, no more to be separated. Soon I shall crown him with this wreath of triumph and my nation will hail him as their Delieverer. Hosanna! they come! they come! On the brow of yonder hill, I already see their banners and the glitter of their spears. I hear their music echoing from the mountain side. Oh God of Israel, thou alone art God, and there is none other!

The curtain is now drawn aside, and Heleon, who represents Jephthah, enters with a sword in his hand, accompanied by the other Pillars.

Heleon — Once more I see my native village and the dwelling-place of my child. Soon shall I greet her, and, in the history of my exploits and the joys of victory, forget all the dangers to which I have been exposed. Beloved Adah! how must your gentle heart now bound with joy. But, here I pause to recall the solemn vow I made when last I stood upon this spot. As I went forth, in the might of Israel's God, to repel the hosts of Ammon, I swore with uplifted arm, that if HE would, without fail, deliver them into my hand, when I returned home in peace, whatsoever should come forth from the doors of my house to meet me, it should be the Lord's and I would offer it up for a burnt-offering.

Now I pause to learn what shall be the victim. The pet lamb

41

of my beloved Adah was wont to run and meet me when I returned from the mountain chase. It were a harsh welcome to my daughter to slay her gentle favorite; yet my oath is registered in heaven. I am becoming anxious. Trumpets, sound again! that Adah may know of my approach and send out some messenger to meet me.

The trampling of feet and music are renewed. The ladies who have remained near the door now move slowly toward Heleon. As his eyes fall upon them, he starts in anguish, cries aloud: Alas, my daughter! and then, falling upon his knees, buries his face in his hands. The ladies approach him and Luna accosts him:

Luna — My father, why this distress?

Heleon — Alas, my daughter!

Luna — What has thy daughter done, to distress thee?

Heleon — Thou hast brought me very low!

Luna — Father, father, what cruel words are these?

Heleon — Thou art one of them that trouble me; for I have opened my mouth to the Lord, and I cannot turn back. Heleon rises, and after a short pause continues slowly and solemnly: Daughter! Beloved and only child! When I went forth at the head of the army of Israel, I felt that in God alone could I hope for victory. Therefore I consecrated myself in solemn prayer to Him. And I vowed a vow, that should I return victorious and in peace, whatsoever should come forth to meet me should be the Lord's — a victim — a burnt offering! Oh my daughter! how little did I anticipate this result! How much better had I perished by the sword of Ammon! Alas, my daughter! my vow is registered in heaven. My soul is perjured. I shall be miserable both in this world and in the next; for I cannot, cannot take thy life.

Luna — My father, if thou hast opened thy mouth unto the Lord, do to me according to that which has proceeded out of thy mouth. Better that I should die, dear father, than thou lose thy soul. Yea, rather better a thousand deaths. I will die, and our people shall see that Adah was worthy to be the daughter of Jephthah, the deliverer of his people.

42

She takes the sword from her father's hand and examines the blade. Then, with a pathetic impulse, she adds:

But oh, my father, in this first hour of your return, while the nation is exulting at your victory, it is hard to die today! I cannot submit my neck to this sword today. Give me a little time to contemplate this awful change and prepare for it. I ask for two months to fit my mind for death. Let me go in the mountains in company with these maidens, for two months, and I will surely return.

Heleon — Go, my daughter, and the God of truth go with thee.

The ladies return to the door while Heleon remains in his place. After a few minutes separation, they return, Jephthah's daughter being crowned with a wreath, and Luna addresses Heleon:

Luna — Father, I am come again, agreeable to my pledge. In the caves of the mountains, in answer to my earnest prayers, I have found resignation and peace. I am come, willing I trust, to fulfill your vow, and give myself a victim. For this purpose, with this wreath that I prepared to celebrate your victory, I am crowned. My father, do not afflict your heart too much at my sacrifice. Be resigned to the will of God. And when you think of me, and remember how willingly I suffered this, to save you from dishonor, do not forget in your anguish at my loss, the splendid triumph God granted you in answer to your vow.

Father — friends — life — farewell. A long, a last farewell.

She folds her arms resignedly, and casts her eyes upward:

Do not delay the fatal blow.

Heleon — My daughter! there is another world, where the errors of this life shall be forgiven, and sorrow lost in universal joy. I will meet you there.

Casts the veil over her face. All present cover their faces with their veils. She instantly throws her veil back upon the floor, they imitating her, and speaks, with great resolution:

Luna — Nay, father, I did not consent to this. I cannot permit my eyes to be covered. I will die in the light.

She again folds her arms and looks upward. He picks up the veil, and, while again casting it over her face, says:

Heleon — My daughter, I cannot strike you while your eyes are fixed upon mine.

She throws it off as before, but with more determination, and says:

Luna — Then I will turn them away from you; I will fix them upon yonder mountain tops, where I found peace. But you shall not put me to death in the dark.

Turns from him and folds her arms as before. He regains the veil, and going behind her says, while he covers her face the third time:

Heleon — Do not disobey me thus, my daughter! It is necessary you should consent to this.

She throws it from her face, but retains the ends of it in her hands grasping it with much force. Turning towards him, with a firm and steady look and voice, she says:

Luna — I declare to you, my father, I will never consent to this. To die with my face covered, like a criminal, would be a mark of perpetual infamy and disgrace — a stain upon my memory. This multitude, who have come to witness my death, would be persuaded that I am suffering the penalty of my own crime. I will not thus be debased, and my name go down to the future dishonored. I die innocent. I die not for myself, but for another, even for you. I die to maintain your integrity — and if you will not suffer me to preserve my good name, upon your head be the penalty, for I will not submit to death at all.

She casts her eyes upward.

Heleon — Let it be so, then. Have your desire.

Here ends the ceremony. Heleon invites the candidate to be seated. If others are to receive the Degree at this meeting, she is requested to witness the ceremony, after which the lecture is given to all. See Chap. VIII for all the lectures.

RUTH

Chapter IV

Sec. 1. The paraphernalia necessary to the Degree of Ruth are: Sheaves and Parcels of Straw; a Sickle, and a Basket of Refreshments.

The room is strewed with Parcels of Straw to represent a barley field.

44

The Degree of Ruth, or the Widow's Degree, comprises the history of Ruth, the Widow of Mahlon the Bethlehemite, who, forsook her native country, princely friends and a beloved home, for the love of God.

The scriptural account of the transaction is contained in the Book of Ruth. The ancient "Degree of the Eastern Star" affords the traditions on which the ceremonial and lectures are based.

Boaz is represented in the dialogue by Philomath; Ruth by Flora; Naomi by Areme; the Overseer by Herald. All the members of the Constellation — both male and female, should take part in the drama, to give it due effect.

Sec. 3. The Candidate being announced by Warder, in the ante-room, as in readiness, by Signal No. 6, Heleon makes Signal No. 7 in reply. The five Correspondents then retire to the ante-room to receive her and Flora thus addresses her:

Flora — My dear Sister. You are about to represent Ruth, that pious woman, the widow of Mahlon the Bethlehemite, who forsook her native country, princely friends and a beloved home for the love of God. Carefully observe whatever passes under your notice, my dear Sister, and let the impressive lessons of this Degree sink deeply into your heart.

Warder repeats the Covenant of Adoption and demands her assent to it. The ladies then enter in company and remain by the door.

Areme, who represents Naomi, addresses Flora, who represents Ruth:

Areme — My daughter, we have nothing left now but to trust in God. Our money is expended; our last morsel of food is consumed; I have called at every house where a friend or relative once resided, and have sought relief, but in vain. My friends do not recognize my claim. My relatives are dead or the few who survive have forgotten me. All my humiliation has been in vain. The Almighty hath dealt very bitterly with me. I pray you then, my daughter, no longer attempt to share my cheerless lot, but rather return to your own princely home and friends, and be happy there. You have already sacrificed too much for me. Go dear Ruth, and leave me to my fate.

Flora — Entreat me not to leave thee or to return from following after thee; for whither thou goest I will go, and where thou lodgest I will lodge; thy people shall be my people, and thy God my God; where thou diest I will die, and there will I be buried; the Lord do so to me and more also, if aught but death part thee and me!

I will go, my mother, into the barley-fields and glean. It cannot be, but that some liberal man among this people may yet take compassion upon our distress and afford me the means of maintaining you; while I have the strength to toil for your subsistence, you shall not suffer want. Give me your blessing, then, my mother, and let me go.

Areme — Nay, my daughter, I will go. Such hardships are not for you. Our long journey from Moab has already exhausted your strength, and you could not endure it. So delicately nurtured as you have been, the hot sun in the barley-fields would overpower you; I am more accustomed to toil and I will go.

Flora — The strength of a good resolution will support me, my mother and the arm of the Almighty will strengthen me. Give me your blessing and let me go.

Areme — The Lord recompense your work and a full reward be given thee of the Lord God of Israel, under whose wings thou art come to trust.

The ladies now move toward the curtain, which is thrown aside, and they behold a representation of a barley-field, in which workmen and gleaners are engaged. Upon the floor appears sheaves and loose straw. The Pillars are observed to be arranging the sheaves — one of them, the Overseer, having a sickle in his hand. Flora picks up a few bits of straw with apparent fatigue, and then rising, speaks, as if to herself:

Flora — I feel that Naomi spake truly. The sun glares upon my head like a sheet of flame. The stubble scorches my feet like coals of fire. My heart begins to sink within me. I feel that I must faint. I will try to return to Naomi. Oh, God of Israel, for whom I have forsaken all things, witness my distress and hear the Widow's cry! Give me help!

Goes near the door and reclines against the wall as if exhausted. Philomath, who represents Boaz, and who has been thus far, in the background, out of view, now comes among the reapers with a basket in his hand, and speaks to the Overseer:

Philomath — It is well. The workmen have done a good task today. Call them around me now and let them partake of the refreshments I have provided.

Observes Ruth:

But what — who — whose damsel is this?

Herald — It is the Moabitish damsel who came back with Naomi, out of the country of Moab — and she said to me, I pray you, let me glean and gather after the reapers, among the sheaves. So she came, and hath continued here, even from the morning until now.

Philomath — She appears to be fatigued. She is quite exhausted.

Herald — Sir, it is plain she has not been accustomed to hardships like these. I observed early this morning, how painfully the stubble scorched her feet, and with what difficulty she gathered up the gleanings. And as the sun came over us, she has dropped more and more, until, like a stricken lily, she bows her head and can do no more. Sir, observe her with those two handfuls of barley; it is all she has gathered today!

Philomath — God has sent her to us that she may find relief. I will invite her to partake of these refreshments.

He advances towards her. As she observes him approaching, she raises her head, and looking towards heaven, speaks as if to herself.

Flora — It is the owner of the field. What should he want of me but to insult and reproach me? O cruel people! shall I not find one friendly soul among you! He takes me to be an intruder — peradventure a thief — and he will drive me from the field. Oh God of Israel, for whom I have forsaken all things, witness now my distress, and hear the Widow's cry! Give me help! Holds up her two handfuls of barley to show him that she is but a poor gleaner, and gazes intently towards heaven. (Philomath comes before her and speaks.)

Philomath — Ruth, it hath been fully showed me all that thou hast done unto thy mother-in-law since the death of thine husband, and how thou hast left thy father and thy mother, and the land of thy nativity, and are come unto a people which thou knewest not heretofore. The Lord recompense thy work, and a full reward be given thee of the Lord God of Israel, under whose wings thou dost trust. Come with me and partake of the refreshments which I have provided for my reapers. They all gather around the basket and partake, accosting one another with cheerful words. After a minute or two Philomath addresses:

Herald, let her glean even among the sheaves, and reproach her not: and let fall also some of the handfuls of purpose for her; and leave them that she may glean them and rebuke her not.

Here ends the ceremony. Heleon invites the candidate to be seated. If others are to receive the Degrees, at this meeting, she is requested to witness the ceremony, after which the lecture is given to all. See Chap. VIII for all the lectures.

ESTHER

Chapter V

Sec. 1. The paraphernalia necessary to the Degree of Esther are, two Crowns, a Scepter, a white Scarf and two Swords.

The room requires no preparation save the curtain.

Sec. 2. The Degree of Esther, or the Wife's Degree comprises the history of Esther, wife and Queen of Ahasuerus, king of Persia. This pious lady offered her crown and life to rescue her people from impending death. The Scriptural account of the transaction is contained in the Book of Esther. The ancient Degree of "The Eastern Star" affords the traditions on which the ceremonial and lectures are founded.

Ahasuerus is represented in the dialogue by Verger; Esther by Hebe; the two guards by Philomath and Herald. All the members of the Constellation, both male and female, should take part in the drama, to give it due effect.

Sec. 3. The Candidate being summoned by Warder, in the ante-room, as in readiness, by Signal No. 6, Heleon makes Signal No. 7 in reply. The five Correspondents then retire to the ante-room to receive her, and Hebe thus addresses her:

Hebe — My Sister, you are about to represent Esther, that heroic woman, the wife and queen of Ahasuerus, who voluntarily periled her crown and life to preserve her nation, the people of God, from impending destruction. Carefully observe whatever passes under your notice and let the impressive lessons of this Degree sink deeply into your heart.

Warder repeats the Covenant of Adoption to her and demands her assent to it. The ladies then enter in company, and remain by the door. Hebe, who represents Esther, then addresses the other Correspondents, who represent her maidens.

Hebe — All now is in readiness for the effort. I have done all I could to prepare for this trial, and nothing remains but to make the attempt. By prayer, and fasting, for three days and nights, I have endeavored to secure the favor of God. For, is it not for his dear sake that I am thus imperiling all that I hold dear? In this cruel edict my life is not attempted; nor should I personally suffer this dreadful penalty. But, Oh my people! the hunted exiles of Judah! doomed nation of God! to what a fate are you exposed? How can I live and see you destroyed? Better that we all perish together, and the faithfulness of death seal the friendship cemented in life.

This is the last day which remains for me to accomplish my purpose, and even now it is full late. I will go in unto the king, which is not according to the law, and if I perish, I perish.

Maidens, robe me for the sacrifice. Give me a garb of purest white and the golden crown upon my head. Peradventure, when the king beholds me thus arrayed, he will be reminded of the solemn vow which, in the years gone by, he made me, and I shall accomplish my purpose.

The attendants tie the white scarf over her left shoulder, so that it crosses her breast to the right side, and place the crown upon her head.

Now, my maidens, let us move forward, and while we approach the gate of the Palace, in which life or death awaits us, let your hearts, with mine, be directed to that Throne whence cometh all our help.

They move slowly forward.

Hebe — Be pleased, Oh Lord, to deliver me: Oh Lord make

49

haste to help me. Withhold not thy tender mercies from me, Oh Lord; let thy loving kindness and thy truth continuously preserve me. Why art thou cast down Oh my soul? and why art thou disquieted within me? hope thou in God: for I shall yet praise him who is the health of my countenance and my God.

Marching two and two they approach the Guards, who are seated in front of the curtain. The Guards rise, cross their swords before her, and Philomath accosts:

Philomath — Back! You cannot pass here. Back! I say. Do you not know that this is the King's palace and that we are his guards?

Hebe — Stand aside! I command you. I am your Queen and will enter. Guards, stand aside.

Philomath — Madam, I recognize you, and respect you, both for your station and your character. Your kindness and affability to all your subjects have endeared your memory throughout the nation. I know that your word here is law. Yet it is at your peril if you enter this place.

To-day is the Grand Council of the Nation. With the King are assembled the Princes and Rulers of the land, and His Majesty will on this occasion, more than all others, be offended at your intrusion. I pray you, Royal Madam, do not pass.

Hebe — Stand aside, I have estimated the peril and I will undertake it. Let me pass!

Herald — Royal Madam, it is an inviolable law of the Palace, that no person shall enter unless summoned by the King, under penalty of death. I entreat you be warned before your blood stains these walls. If you enter, it is to certain death.

Hebe — Let me pass, and no longer delay my enterprise. The responsibility be upon my own head.

Herald — Pass then, and may God protect you!

The curtain is here drawn aside and exhibits the Grand Council. The King is seated; the other Officers are standing on his right and left; he wears a crown upon his head and bears in his right hand a scepter; as the ladies enter he is speaking to those around him:

Verger — As to this accursed nation, let their destruction be sharp and sure. See that no lingering slaughter or protracted

50

death makes their fate uncertain; but in one day, yea if it be possible, in one hour, let the sword reach them, old and young, until not one be left. Then shall my kingdom —

At this instant his eye falls upon Hebe, and he abruptly pauses. He rises to his feet, his countenance expressing the greatest surprise and anger. He speaks:

Verger — What means this intrusion? Guards, upon your lives be this act. Are my strictest orders thus to be disregarded? Were it my mother, she should die. Take her at once to the courtyard and put her to death.

The Guards rush upon her and seize her by each hand to lead her away. She accompanies them a few paces, then snatches her hands from theirs, turns towards the King and makes two parts of the Hailing Sign of Esther, her eyes being directed towards heaven. (See Tuilleur.) The King speaks quickly and in a softened tone:

Verger — Stop Guards, release her. Return to your posts. Esther, my Queen, approach hither, and receive my pardon.

She advances to him and places her right hand upon the top of the sceptre, which he extends toward her.

Verger — What wilt thou, Queen Esther? and what is thy request? It shall even be granted thee to the half of the kingdom.

Here ends the ceremony. Heleon invites the candidate to be seated. If others are to receive the Degree at this meeting, she is requested to witness the ceremony; after which, the lecture is given to all. See Chapter VIII for all the lectures.

MARTHA

Chapter VI

Sec. 1. This Degree is communicated without ceremonial; and to all the Candidates simultaneously.

This was found necessary, as the principal male character in the dialogue would necessarily have represented the Lord Jesus Christ, whom to attempt thus to impersonate would be blasphemous. The well-informed lecturer will be able, however, to make an impression upon the minds of the Candidates but little short of that made by a dramatic rehearsal. The Covenant of Adoption must be repeated to the Candidate as in the other Degrees, and her assent demanded to it.

Sec. 2. The Degree of Martha, or the Sister's Degree, comprises the history of Martha, the sister of Lazarus and friend to the Saviour. This faithful lady, oppressed with the loss of all she held dear on earth, could yet look up through her sorrows to Christ and profess an unshaken reliance upon his words. The Scriptural account of the transaction is contained in the Book of John. The ancient Degree of the "Eastern Star" affords the tradition on which the lectures are founded. See Chapter VIII for all the Lectures.

ELECTA

Chapter VII

Sec. 1. The paraphernalia necessary to the Degree of Electa are a Sword, a black Cross, a bundle of Clothing, a Purse, and a Dish covered with Food.

Sec. 2. The Degree of Electa, or the Christian Martyr's Degree, comprises the history of Electa, the Martyr of Christ, and the wife of the Past Grand Master of Masons. She sacrificed all things in testimony of her love for Christ. The only Scriptural allusion to Electa — and this is but brief and indistinct — is in the Second Epistle of John. The ancient Degree of "Eastern Star" affords the traditions on which the ceremonial and lectures are founded.

St. John is represented in the dialogue by Herald; Electa by Areme. No others need take part in the drama of this Degree.

Sec. 3. The Candidate being announced by Warder, in the ante-room, as in readiness, by Signal No. 6, Heleon makes Signal No. 7 in reply. The five Correspondents then retire to the ante-room and Areme thus addresses her:

Areme — My dear Sister: You are about to represent Electa, that renowned lady, the friend of St. John and wife of Gaius, Past Grand Master of Masons. She sacrificed all things for the love she bore to the Saviour. Carefully observe whatever passes under your notice, my dear Sister, and let the impressive lessons of this Degree sink deeply into your heart.

Warder repeats the Covenant of Adoption to her and demands her assent to it. The ladies then enter in company and stand some distance to the right or left of the door. Herald, who is on the inner side of the veil, is heard as if reading from a letter he has just received:

Herald — That the new Religion be crushed out from every nation where the Roman rule prevails! that its votaries, one and all, be required to renounce it, or be mercilessly sacrificed! That the Roman soldiers — ah, cruel band! — visit the dwelling of every suspected Christian, and see that he acquit himself of the suspicion by trampling upon the Cross! Take notice, Most Worshipful Grand Master, and govern yourself accordingly.

Ah, cruel Emperor! Ah, hapless people! Alas, the persecuted Church of Christ, what will avail you now? People of the living Saviour, whither now will you flee? Is there no rest but the grave, for the friends of Jesus?

And you, pious Electa, true-hearted Sister in Christ, delight of all who love the Lord, what will be your fate, now? How will you sustain this dreadful trial? Many will deny Christ in these latter days of persecution, and purchase a miserable life by denying Him who gave His life as a ransom for many. Will your name be added to that traitorous band? I tremble to consider it. Yet, how many, who have been devoted to Him, in the day of ease and quiet, afterwards, when affliction or persecution ariseth for the Word's sake, are offended.

I am oppressed with anxiety concerning this woman. If Electa is found to shrink under this calamity, who, then, will be faithful? Aged and infirm as I am, under the yoke of five score years, I will arise and go to her dwelling, to satisfy my mind that she is faithful. And that she may not easily recognize me until I have communicated this message, I will disguise myself in the garb of a Roman soldier, the bitterest enemy of the Cross, and thus present myself at her door.

The curtain is now drawn aside and exhibits Herald armed with a Sword. He walks slowly as if with weariness and pain, towards the door of entrance.   Arrived there, he halts and soliloquizes:

The task is more than I had reckoned it.   Had the distance been but a little greater, I could not have accomplished it.   Five score years have done their work too faithfully for such journeys as these.   I will apply for admission.

He knocks.

Dusty and disguised as I am in this garb, Electa will surely be unable to recognize me.   I am quite exhausted.

He leans upon the sword in his left hand by the side of the door.   The ladies approach him.

Areme, who represents Electa — Observes him narrowly and halts.   She soliloquizes:

Areme — A soldier! A Roman soldier! The butchers of Christ, and the insatiable ravagers of his flock — what does he here?   Why has he chosen to call upon me?   But my duty is plain, whatever may be his motives I will dispense to him Christian hospitality.   I perceive he is very aged and infirm.   He appears overcome with heat and fatigue.   I will hesitate no longer.   Perhaps God has sent him here for his soul's good.

She goes to him and takes him kindly by the hand.

My aged Brother, in the name of the Lord Jesus Christ, welcome to my dwelling.   Let it be your home while you tarry here. Enter.   The liberal hand of providence has endowed me richly with the means of hospitality.   Enter, and, as if sent by Him, partake freely of His benefits.

She leads him a little way and seats him.

Let me refresh you with water.

She brings him water of which he drinks.

The day is hot, the roads are hard and dusty — your journey has been too great for you.   It was often so with our blessed Saviour, who, in his ministry, used to pass this way when I was but a little child.   Hungry and thirsty and wearied as you are, he has often realized in this very dwelling how bitter is the lot of man!

Now, my Brother, you seem refreshed; the color mounts to your cheek and light comes again to your eye.   Does the name of

Christ bring such animation to your soul? Ah, I have experienced its benefits.

Cheer up, then, cheer up, aged friend! There shall nothing be wanting for your comfort here. The love of Christ constraineth me and whatever I have is your own. Speak, brother, and command me what I shall do for you?

Herald — I am hungry. Since the morning watch I have not broken bread. Yet a few crusts will suffice me and I will be thankful.

Areme — No crusts from me. While Electa has an abounding providence for her own support, the wayfarer whom Christ may direct hither shall not have crusts.

She presents him a dish covered with food.

Take of the best my house affords and welcome.

After a few minutes she brings him a cup of wine.

Accept this cup of the richest wine my house affords. May its generous flavor give you new strength and prove, at least, the earnest of your welcome.

After he has drunk she continues.

But what further token of hospitality can I offer you. Speak, Brother, and command me, what I shall do for you.

Herald — Draws forth an empty purse and hands to her.

My purse is empty — my home is far away. I have but little strength to labor for money. Give me a few farthings to enable me to reach the next village and I will be thankful.

Areme — Nay not a few farthings.

She fills the purse as if with gold.

But rather let me furnish you the means for your entire journey. And when you shall once again reach that distant home, may you find its loved ones all in health and prepared to meet you.

She returns him the purse.

But all your wants are not yet supplied. Speak, again, Brother, and command me. What shall I do for you?

Herald — My raiment is old and worn. Yet I shall not much longer need a covering, therefore, if your husband or servants have any cast-off garments you would bestow upon me, I would be thankful.

Areme — Not so, my Brother, I will deal more bountifully with you than you ask.

She presents him with a bundle as if filled with clothing.

Here is the best in our wardrobe, and may they give you comfort and warmth until you reach your distant home and friends. But is there not something further I can do for you? Think: I should feel loth to know that any left me in distress while I have the means for their relief.

Herald — No, kind lady, nothing further. All that I was in want of has been supplied me, and for your generous bounty, believe me, I am thankful. But now that I am refreshed and able to deliver my message, I will inform you what is my business in this part of the country. The Emperor at Rome has been pleased to issue an edict, to the effect "that the new Religion be crushed out from every nation where the Roman rule prevails! That its votaries, one and all, be required to renounce it or be mercilessly sacrificed! that the Roman soldiers visit the dwelling of every suspected Christian, and see that he acquit himself of the suspicion by trampling upon the cross." I have, therefore, come to inquire of you, as of one who is best acquainted throughout this region, are there any Christians amongst your neighbors, and if so, to demand their names.

He looks her steadily in the face. She returns his look with a surprised air, but makes him no reply. After a brief pause he continues:

Madam, there is something suspicious in your silence. Why should you hesitate to reply? Are there any Christians in *your* family? Your manner would seem to indicate it. Give me their names, or you will suffer the penalty as though you were one in person.

He again pauses and looks in her face as before; but she makes him no reply. He rises and continues:

Madam, can it be that you are a Christian? One so wealthy, so accomplished, so hospitable! Can it be possible that you have subjected yourself to such a horrid doom? But no, there is a means of escape; there is a method, easy and sure, by which this terrible punishment may be avoided. Madam, you have been kind to me in my hour of distress, and I will show you that I am grateful.

He draws from his pocket a small black Cross.

According to the terms of the law, whoever is suspected of being a Christian, may acquit himself of the suspicion by trampling on the Cross. You will preserve your life, your property and the lives of your husband and children by casting this upon the floor and putting your foot upon it. Then I will go forth and declare that you have submitted to the law and renounced the Christian religion. Take it.

All this time she has not ceased to look him sternly and indignantly in the face. But now, she takes the Cross from his hand, her countenance changes to tenderness, she presses the Cross ardently to her lips and bosom; then she speaks.

Areme — Sir, are you a demon in the form of humanity, that you strive to imperil my soul with these allurements? and think you I am terrified with your threats? Why, what is there in all you have said to move me? Have I not lived fifteen years daily expecting, waiting, desiring this message, and shall it shake me now?

You ask me, too, if I am a Christian? and you profess to be astonished to discover that I am a Christian; did I not meet you at my threshold and welcome you in the name of Jesus Christ? Have I not fed you and tended upon your wants for the sake of Jesus Christ? What was there in you or in me, independent of my faith in the Crucified One, which should prompt me to such actions?

Cease, then, your allurements, and spare me the further recital of my perils. I am a Christian. This family, one and all, are Christians. One and all we have long been prepared to render up all things for the sake of Him who gave all things to us — go on, then, and do your duty. Spare no part of it for the remembrance of my hospitality, and God, for Christ's sake, will enable me to do mine.

She places herself in the position of the Sign of Electa. (See Tuilleur.) Herald lays aside his sword and speaks kindly to her:

Herald — Electa, my Sister, tried and true, look upon me again. Do you not know me? I am John.

Areme — John! it is indeed! Oh Sir, how could you try my feelings in this cruel manner?

Herald — That I might learn the strength of your religious

character. I confess, my dear Sister, that I feared this alarming and most unexpected intelligence might shake your faith, and I disguised myself in this manner to try you unobserved; but all is clear now, your gold is altogether pure; you are the fairest among ten thousand and altogether lovely.

Electa, in a few days you may expect that this scene which has tried you so, will be realized. The soldiers will come and the rest will follow. I see in store for you a terrible sacrifice and a cruel death. But you need no pity. Your reward is in heaven, and soon shall I meet you there to rehearse the events which now are nigh at hand.

Electa, we will Masonically embalm your religious fortitude and your triumphant death. As Grand Master of Masons I will institute a Degree to be entitled after your name, which shall perpetuate your history among us while there is a woman's eye to weep or a man's heart to feel for the sorrows of suffering virtue.

Here ends the ceremony. Heleon invites the Candidate to be seated. If others are to receive the Degrees at this meeting, she is requested to remain and witness the ceremony, after which the lecture is given to all. See Chapter VIII for all the lectures.

THE LECTURES

Chapter VIII

Sec. 1. The Lectures which follow, when combined with the references to the Tuilleur, which accompany them, constitute all the instructions that is thought necessary to offer in this volume. But those portions of Scripture which give the histories of Jephthah's Daughter, Ruth, Esther, and Martha, may be considered essential parts of these Lectures; and the enlightened Mason who would attempt to interest the female mind upon this subject, must familiarize himself, first of all, with the inspired word or he will scarcely succeed in his effort.

It should be understood that none of the traditions of the Eastern Star contradict the text of Scripture. They, indeed, extend the Scriptural history, and they throw important light upon the passages referred to — like, furthermore, they may be found opposed to the opinions of some modern commentators — particularly those that relate to the fate of Jephthah's Daughter, etc. — but there is no shade of discrepancy between these Lectures and the generally-received understanding of the Bible. Of this, the pious Christian may be well assured, even in advance of a perusal.

Sec. 2. Previous to the establishment of the American Adoptive Rite, it was the inherent privilege — in many places largely exercised — of every Master Mason to communicate the Degree of the "Eastern Star" without any ceremonial, but under the following restrictions:

1. Five or more ladies must be present at its communication. Men alone could not receive it.

2. They must be of the age of 18 years or upwards.

3. They must be the wives, daughters, sisters or widows of Master Masons in good standing.

4. They must give their assent in advance to the following pledge: "So many of you, Ladies, as do pledge your sacred honor as women, forever to keep the secrets of this Degree, raise your right hand!"

5. As many Master Masons in good standing may be present at this communication as choose. No particular number is requisite.

But they must give their assent in advance to the following pledge: "So many of you, Brothers, as do pledge your sacred honor as Masons, to communicate this Degree only in the manner and under the circumstances in which you are now to receive it, raise your right hand!"

The inherent right which Master Masons possessed, to communicate the Degree under the above-named restrictions, remains forever unchanged, nor does the Supreme Constellation presume to interfere with it. Those who come lawfully into possession of this volume, may, if they think proper, make it the basis of such communication, avoiding, however, the imparting of any of the Ritual of the Constellation in so doing.

The Lectures in this Chapter, when amplified by the Scriptural history appropriate to each, will enable them to make such communication pleasant and instructive to the parties authorized to receive it. Nothing but good can grow out of this course, and the healthful spread of the Adoptive Rite may, and in many places doubtless will depend upon communicating the original Degree in the former manner, as essential to the awakening of a dormant interest in the subject itself.

Members of a Constellation who may communicate the Eastern Star according to the original method, as above authorized, are required to forward a list of the names of females thus instructed to the V. E. Grand Secretary of the Supreme Constellation.

Sec. 3. The first Degree having been conferred, as described in the preceding Chapters, Heleon will address the Initiate or Initiates with the following Lecture on Jephthah's Daughter:

My Sister!

All the great lessons of human life, worthy of our contemplation, are evolved from sorrow and distress. All true heroism, whether in man or in woman, has been manifested from the depths of grief. It is in the night of affliction only that the stars of faith and devotion are most visible to the eye.

All the lessons of the Eastern Star acknowledge this great truth, that the way of the Cross is the way of Life. The histories of Jephthah's Daughter, of Ruth, of Esther, of Martha and of Electa were but examples of this — living, beautiful examples — and as such they all demand, amidst our admiration, sympathy and tears.

The unnumbered woes that in all ages have embittered the lot of woman, who can tell? What eye has marked her tears? What ear has heard her sighs, her words of woe. In her still and un-romantic life she has endured such anguish as the heedless world knew not of. Yet there was an Eye that marked, an Ear that heard, a Heart that heeded her expressions of sorrow. The Divine Friend has melted at the view of her distress, and here in this Book of Books, the Divine hand has recorded many tokens of her bitter lot. It is these sad histories that form the foundation of our Order. Four of them, extended by tradition, and beautified and made impressive by ceremonies, constitute the Scriptural portion of the American Adoptive Rite, to which the traditions of Masonry have added a fifth, even more beautiful, if possible, than the others.

My Sister!

We are happy, in these Lectures, to offer you such lessons of devotion, self sacrifice, free-will offering, faith and Christian love, as will, if rightly understood, serve as models to yourself, in all circumstances of trial and distress to which you may be exposed. The first is that of Jephthah's Daughter.

Jephthah was the Judge and Governor of Israel, a pious man, a devoted father, and exemplary Mason. For the age in which he lived, he was the pattern of prudence and virtue.

Being called forth to fight the battles of his country, he first of all invoked the aid of Jehovah, to whom all his supplications were addressed. He prayed for assistance from the Hand Almighty, and in accordance with the religious and Masonic usages of his day, made a vow, that, if God would assuredly give him the victory, and return him to his home in safety, he would offer up as a burnt offering whatever should first meet him coming from his house. This vow, though disastrous in its results, was offered up from the purest motives.

Thus invoked, it pleased God to accept the petition, and to grant the victory. The foe met a disastrous defeat; Israel was saved, and the pious General returned homeward, crowned with honors, and full of pious joy.

Arrived in sight of his dwelling, the victorious Chieftain paused; for now the consequences of his oath crowded upon his mind. He asked himself what would be the victim? His daughter's lamb, the pet of the sportive hours, it was that which he had had chiefly in view in making his oath; but even that, his love for his daughter made it a painful duty to slay. Not long, however, was he in suspense; for, aroused by all her love for her father, and her gratitude to God, and rendered impatient by his halting so near the dwelling, the joyful girl, ignorant of his vow, and heedless of the customs of her country, which forbade such exposure, seized her instruments of music, and with singing and dancing passed that fatal door and ran towards him.

The stricken father fell to the earth, rending his clothes and groaning in the agony of his heart, Alas, my daughter!

How cruelly was that current of joy checked! The song of

triumph ceased! The timbrels were cast aside, and Jephthah's daughter, informed of her father's rash vow, turned away to commune with her heart.

Should she refuse to submit to this awful fate? The laws would protect her; public opinion would sustain her in her natural desire to live. Why should she die? Innocent of any harm, at that age, of all others, when life seems most golden and hopeful, why should she pay the penalty of her father's rashness, and submit to such a death.

But then other thoughts possessed her mind. She was a Mason's daughter, and well she knew that a Freemason, of all earthly treasures, prizes his religious honor. His oath was registered in heaven, perhaps God had granted him that splendid victory in consequence of it; and it demanded a victim. Should she refuse to be that victim, her father was perjured before God and Man, and could hope for nothing but judgment in the world to come.

She turned to him and said she would submit. She, who so much needed sympathy and pity, forgot her own distress in the contemplation of his. · She reminded him of his sacred calling, of God's acceptance of him heretofore, of the shortness of life, and the certainty of heaven, where they should meet again, and be happy forever more.

But one request she made — it was hard to die, but oh, how hard to die then. In that joy with which the day had opened, in that first rush of national triumph, she could not consent to die then. She asked that she might be spared two months that she might go up and down upon the mountains with her companions and prepare herself for her fate.

The time being ended, she returned to her father and suffered death according to his vow. And it became a custom in Israel, that the daughters of Israel went yearly to lament her, four days in a year. This is the foundation of this Degree.

In immediate connection with her death, a circumstance occurred, preserved in the tradition of this Degree, while it affords us the origin of the DAUGHTER'S HAILING SIGN, throws much light upon the character of this amiable young woman.

The last embrace having been given, the last farewell spoken, her father threw a veil over her face and drew his sword to consummate the sacrifice. She threw it indignantly back, declaring it was infamous to be put to death in the dark, as if she were a criminal suffering for her own offenses, and that she would never submit to it. Her father the second time veiled her, assuring her that he could not strike the fatal blow while she looked upon him. At this declaration, she again cast it off, but turned from him and fixed her eyes resolutely upwards, asserted her unchangeable refusal to be veiled. Nevertheless, Jephthah the third time attempted to cover her eyes, whereupon she seized the veil firmly in her hands, and in the most solemn manner assured him that rather than suffer the imputation which it would cast upon her memory, she would refuse, altogether, to die for his vow, and the penalty of his perjury might rest upon his own head. This decisive declaration ended the contest, and she was suffered to fall with her eyes fixed to the last, upon the heavens.

JEPHTHAH'S DAUGHTER

Judges XI, 35

Father, father, the joyful minstrel sung —
  Lo, glad I come with timbrel and with dance:
Hail, father, hail! thine arm in God was strong.
  Hail, God of Israel, Israel's sure defense.
      Hosanna! Hosanna!
     Thus the Minstrel sung.

Father, father! th' astonished daughter cried —
  What grief is this? What means this sign of wo?
Dust on thy head! Thy grey hairs floating wide!
  That look of horror on each soldier's brow —
      Bewailing, bewailing —
     Thus the Daughter cried.

Father, father! the maid devoted said —
  If thus I'm doomed, if thus thy vow has gone,
Oh turn not back! there's hope amidst the dead,
  None for the perjured — let thy will be done,
      Hosanna! Hosanna!
     Thus the Maiden said.

Father, father! the doomed one meekly spoke —
Be strong thy hand, be resolute thy heart —
To heaven's re-union I will joyful look,
And with a blessing on thy head depart.
Farewell! farewell!
Thus the Doomed One spoke.

Sec. 4. The second Degree having been conferred, as described in the preceding Chapters, Heleon will address the Initiate or Initiates with the following Lecture of Ruth:

My Sister!

Mahlon, a Jew of the city of Bethlehem, had been driven by extreme famine into the country of Moab, where he continued for ten years, and until the period of his death. He married a woman of that country, named Ruth, and being a pious, God-fearing man, and withal a devoted Freemason, his heart was set upon converting his wife to the faith which formed the joy of his own soul. In this he was entirely successful. Ruth became deeply pious, and vied with him in a worship as ennobling as it was pure.

In process of time, as already mentioned, he died. Calling his wife to him, and communicating his last wishes, he exhorted her not to remain in that heathen land, where none could care for her soul, but to seek the country of Judah, and the city of Bethlehem, whence he had formerly emigrated, and there, amidst the people of God, to hold fast to that faith and worship which would insure her eternal felicity after death. To this, his dying request, she cheerfully assented and pledged herself accordingly.

Having seen the grass springing upon the grave of one with whom she had enjoyed so much happiness, she departed for the land of Judah. Forbidden by law to remove any of her property, which was great, or to sell her possessions, which were large, she hesitated not to forsake them, and to go, poor and lonely, with no companionship save that of her aged mother-in-law, to a land of strangers, a people of whom she had hitherto known nothing, save that they were the nation of God, and of her deceased husband.

They treated her unworthily, whether we consider her own holy errand or their national character. She went meekly from door to door, but found none who could give her a place to rest, or food to eat, and, so soon as the small sum of money she had brought from Moab was exhausted, she began to be in extreme want. The care of her aged mother-in-law likewise fell upon her, and she know not how to provide.

It was the season of barley-harvest, and as Ruth was too inexperienced in labor to gain employment from others, she sought, in the gleanings of the field, to find food for herself and her helpless friend. She went into the field of Boaz, a wealthy man of that city, and began to glean.

But it was not long until she found that she had over-rated her strength. The blazing sun of the country struck almost into her brain. The heated stubble parched her tender feet. Faint with hunger, exhausted with fatigue, overpowered with heat, the unfortunate woman was fain to yield to despair and cease her efforts. All her toil until noon had only yielded her two poor handfuls of barley.

The owner of the field — Boaz by name — was as famed for his liberality as for his wealth. He, too, was a Mason, and had long tutored himself by the sublime principles of that Order, of which he was an honored member, to divide his bread with the suffering poor. To afford succor to the distressed was one of the prime joys of his existence, and none knew him but 'to honor his name, and to invoke blessings upon his head.

Coming into the field that day to bring refreshments to his laborers his eyes soon singled out the hapless widow, gleaning there, and he asked of his overseer, in tones of pity, "Who is that?" For she was reclining beneath a fig tree, nearly fainting, unable to toil longer or to return to the city.

She stood with her eyes directed upwards, her hands clasping the poor returns of her labor, her thoughts wandering to the distant country of her birth, the place of her former happiness and ease.

Boaz, upon learning from his overseer, that she was a stranger and poor, and that the task that she had attempted was too onerous for her strength, went at once to her relief, forced a bounteous hospitality upon her, and animating her, not less with kind words than substantial gift, imparted new life to her almost hopeless heart.

And here a circumstance occurred, preserved in the traditions of this Degree, which, while it affords us the origin of the WIDOW's HAILING SIGN, is in itself a touching and beautiful incident.

Beholding Boaz approaching her, and judging by his dress and manner that he was the owner of the field, she at once decided in her own mind, that his purpose was to drive her insultingly from the field, as an intruder and a thief. Therefore, raising herself erect, she held up her two parcels as a token that she was an honest gleaner, and no thief, and continued to gaze steadily upwards, as though pleading with God against the inhumanity of man.

Boaz, after seeing that her immediate wants were supplied, privately instructed the overseer to protect her from any annoyance or reproach from the laborers, and to take parcels from the sheaves and let them fall in her way, that she might gather as much as she would. The Sacred historian informs us, further, that not long afterwards, he married her, and thus the poor gleaner and disconsolate widow was transformed into the most honored matron of the nation. For, tracing her genealogy, we learn that she became the grandmother of David, the father of Solomon, through whose mighty line Jesus Christ, according to the flesh, came.

RUTH

Ruth II, 5

From Moab's hills the stranger comes,
　By sorrow tried, widowed by death;
She comes to Judah's goodly homes,
　Led by the trusting hand of faith.
Ye friends of God, a welcome lend
　The fair and virtuous Ruth to-day;
A cheerful heart and hand extend,
　And wipe the widow's tears away.

She leaves her childhood's home, and all
　That brothers, friends and parents gave;

The flowery fields, the lordly hall,
  The green sod o'er her husband's grave;
Ye friends of God, a welcome lend
  The fair and virtuous Ruth to-day;
A cheerful heart and hand extend,
  And wipe the widow's tears away.

She leaves the gods her people own —
  Soulless and weak, they're hers no more;
JEHOVAH, He is God alone,
  And HIM her spirit will adore.
Ye friends of God, a welcome lend
  The fair and virtuous Ruth to-day;
A cheerful heart and hand extend,
  And wipe the widow's tears away.

At Bethlehem's gates the stranger stands;
  All friendless, poor and wanting rest;
She waits the cheer of loving hands
  And kindred hearts that God has blest.
Ye friends of His a welcome lend
  The fair and virtuous Ruth to-day;
A cheerful heart and hand extend,
  And wipe the widow's tears away.

Sec. 5. The Third Degree having been conferred, as described in the preceding Chapters, Heleon will address the Initiate or Initiates with the following Lecture of Esther:

My Sister!

Ahasuerus, the King of Persia, reigned from India even to Ethiopia over a hundred and twenty-seven provinces. His laws were stern and inexorable; the usages of his nation were cruel; the manners of his time fierce and barbarous. Yet this King was noted for his sense of justice, and his regard for truth was above all things, admirable. He was withal, a Mason, and prized its code of morality as the best standard of right and wrong, with which, in the absence of the true religion, he had ever become acquainted.

It was a period of the greatest adversity in the history of the Jews. The people of God were exiles in a foreign land. By the rivers of Babylon, there they sat down; yea they wept when they remembered Zion. Yet they trusted in God, who, for their sins had given them into the hands of their enemies; and they hoped he would yet have compassion on them and restore them to their native land.

Among the most pious of this unfortunate people was a young woman, Esther by name, an orphan, who, when her father and mother were taken from her by death, had been brought up by her cousin, Mordecai, in the love and fear of God. This lady was as talented as she was fair and beautiful and it pleased God, through her, to work out a great deliverance for his people.

Poor and humble as she was, her remarkable beauty attracted the favor of the King, and he made her his wife. His affection increased, by the charms of her piety, virtue and talents until the confidence he reposed in her extended to a share in his kingdom. He made her his Queen, entrusted her with the secrets of state, and consulted her in every emergency that occurred. Her matchless ability were entirely equal to the demand, and she became famed throughout the kingdom for wisdom, prudence, and devotion to her responsible charge.

The King, in his gratitude for such services, made frequent declarations of his attachment to her, and the readiness and liberality with which he would acknowledge it whenever demanded. He vowed to her, that no sacrifice would be deemed by him too great for this end, even though it involved the half of his kingdom; and he instructed her, in the event of her wishing to claim this promise, to clothe herself in the apparel of her station, — the white silken robes and the crown royal of the Queen, and thus attired, to come boldly before him. And he swore, with arm uplifted to JEHOVAH — that God whom his Masonic instructor had taught him to adore as supreme, — that wherever he might be, or in whatever business engaged, if she would appeal to him in this manner, he would grant her request, be it what it might, even to the half of his kingdom.

About eight years after their union, and while she was yet in the height of his favor, the public indignation became aroused against the Jewish people, and King Ahasuerus was induced to issue a law, that upon a certain day specified, all Jews, both young and old, little children and women, should be destroyed and their property taken as a spoil by their enemies. The fact of this law being passed was speedily communicated to Esther by her cousin, Mordecai, who likewise told her of the great mourning which had followed its announcement to the Jews, and how they were fasting, weeping and wailing, and that many of them lay in sackcloth and ashes. And he pleaded with her that she was now the only hope left to Israel, having, perhaps, been called of God to the kingdom for this very end.

Esther resolved to release them. Her station as Queen, and the favor she enjoyed as counsellor to the King, might well exonerate her from such a task; as in effect it shielded her from the operations of the law. But her love for the Jews, her sense of duty towards God, and the tender compassion aroused within her heart by the recital of their distresses, kindled there a holy determination, that she would rescue them, or share their fate. She prepared for the dangerous attempt, by fasting and prayer for three successive days and nights.

Then all pale with hunger and anticipation, she commanded her maidens to attire her in her queenly apparel, and so, crowned with the crown royal, she betook herself to the palace of the King.

It was the day of a Grand Council, when all the Lords of the kingdom, the Princes and Rulers had met together at the King's command, and the palace gates were shut. The guards instructed her of this, and that, by a law of the palace, whoever should come in unto the King, into the inner-court, not being called, should be put to death. And they warned her that this law applied to the highest as well as the lowest of the nation.

Esther was not deterred by this intelligence, which, truly, she had known before, but bade the guards give her admittance as having prepared her mind to meet this peril, that she might fulfill the great object of her mission. Whereupon they, though unwillingly, suffered her to enter to what they reasonably supposed was her certain death; so, entering through the great folding-doors of the inner-court, she stood before the King.

Ahasuerus sat crowned in royal magnificence upon the throne of his kingdom. Around him was gathered all that could add dignity to his state and give him the highest sense of his own importance. His will was the supreme law to those thousands whose mandates, in turn, ruled the millions of his subjects in the vast territories under his sway. All looked to him as to a being whose breath was their death or life, and waited but to know his faintest wishes to obey them. Was this a time for this pale and trembling woman to violate the strictest law of his person, and to defy him in the presence of his very kingdom?

As the eyes of the multitude fell upon her, the greatest astonishment and consternation prevailed. The King himself arose in his wrath and called loudly to ask why this intrusion was permitted? Upon being informed that the Queen had been warned of her danger, and fully instructed in regard to the law of the palace, he commanded the guards to lead her forth and execute the law upon her without delay.

Trembling with the sense of her peril, alarmed at the frowning countenance of the multitude around, and shuddering under the fearful wrath of the King, Esther had barely strength to place her hand alternately upon her crown and the top of her robe, to remind him of his oath, then sank nearly lifeless to her knees.

The mute appeal smote the King's heart more forcibly than words. He remembered his vow. He recalled all her devotion to him and her labor in behalf of the kingdom. He cast aside the unworthy anger that had possessed him at her intrusion, and called her kindly to him, extended the golden sceptre towards her, that by touching it, she might, in accordance with the customs of the country, secure his pardon. She obeyed his command, and then, seating her by his side upon the throne, he said to her: — What wilt thou? — and declared publicly he would grant her request even to the half of his kingdom.

Your attention is particularly called here to a portion of this scene which, while it affords us the origin of the WIFE's HAILING SIGN, serves to impress upon our minds the important fact of the King's vow to Esther. She reminded him of his oath by touching her crown and robe, with which he had enjoined her to invest herself preparatory to claiming his promise; and she secured a pardon by touching the golden sceptre, which he extended to her.

From Scriptural history we learn, that her mission was entirely successful; the King granted her request; spared the Jewish people; destroyed all their enemies, and advanced Esther to honors, even higher than before.

ESTHER

Esther V, 3

Queen of Persia's broad domain,
  Why this anguish and despair!
Blending tears like falling rain —
  Sighs and words of hopeless prayer!

Round thee stands a waiting train,
  Wealth and beauty, rank and power;
All to bring relief in vain,
  Queen of sadness in this hour.

For a voice has gone abroad,
  Stern and fearful, filled with doom;
Israel's exiles to the sword,
  Sword and brand to Israel's home.

Lo, that high expressive brow!
  Was there e'er a heart so true?
Hark what words the purpose show —
  I will save or perish too.

To the sovereign I will haste;
  Robe your Queen in purity;
Crown me as in triumphs past;
  Maidens to the Throne with me.

Queen, thy holy aim is won, —
  God o'errules the stern decree,
Sends a pardon from the throne,
  Israel saves, and honors thee!

Sec. 6. The Fourth Degree having been communicated, as described in the preceding Chapters, Heleon will address the Initiate or Initiates with the following Lecture of Martha:

My Sister!

Lazarus, a citizen of Bethany, had two sisters, Martha and Mary, who were his housekeepers, and for whose support he labored diligently in his vocation. The three had been favored to attend the administration of Jesus Christ, and had become his first disciples in Bethany. Their home was a welcome shelter to Christ whenever he visited Bethany, and amidst the opposition of their friends and the sneers of their enemies, they openly defended His cause and protected its votaries. Lazarus was a Mason, and a man of standing and respectability in the community in which he lived.

Not long before the closing scenes of Christ's ministry a circumstance occurred upon which this Degree is founded. On a certain occasion, when Christ was absent from Bethany, engaged in the active duties of His calling, Lazarus was taken suddenly and violently ill. The afflicted sisters, confident in the power of the Lord Jesus to restore him, sent to him an urgent message to come to their relief, and the words of the letter were, "Lord, behold, he whom thou lovest is sick."

The Saviour was easily found by the messenger, but, for reasons which afterwards appeared, He did not attend the summons. The messenger returned to inform the sisters that their friend, in whom they had placed such reliance, refused their request, and that they must seek for other aid. But there was no other aid. Death had already grasped its victim with a strong hand, and would not let him go. Amidst the regrets of the community, the sorrows of friends, the tears of the Masonic Brotherhood, and the profound despair of the sisters, Lazarus died.

Well might those afflicted women find a cause for despair. Their brother, their only protector, dead; their Saviour, when of all times in the history of their acquaintance, He was most desired, absent; their faith amidst the scorn of their friends, outraged; little wonder would it have been, had those sisters repudiated their attachment to Christ and joined in the popular outcry against Him, that he was an imposter.

But, amidst their night of affliction, no such token of unfaithfulness was manifested by either of them. Martha steadfastly declared to those around her, that her trust in Christ was unshaken; that, though he might forsake her, she would never forsake him; and though she should die with grief she would die in hope. And so declared her sister.

In the utterance of such sentiments as these, yet bowed down with the weight of sorrow and despair, four days were passed by those sisters, and the world began to forget the dead man in the obscurity of his sepulchre. No tidings of their Lord, — no visit, or message, or word of sympathy.

But at the close of the fourth day, as the sun was going down beyond the hills of Judah, there was a rumor that the Master was coming again to Bethany. Martha heard it and at once there was kindled up in her bosom all that ardor of faith that had distinguished her as a Christian, and the love that had sustained her amidst the contempt of the world. · She ran swiftly from the house, through the village, and forgetting all things at the sight of her Divine Friend, fell at his feet and wept there. She looked upwards, and, through her tears, sought the expression of his face as it beamed upon her.

There was a gentle smile there, a smile of such love as none but Jesus could feel, yet withal a look of heartfelt sympathy, tender, gracious and Oh, how comforting. His face beamed with emotion, such as during those four weary days would have yielded her inexpressible consolation.

She cried aloud, "Lord! if thou hadst been here, my brother had not died. But I know that even now, whatsoever Thou wilt ask of God, God will give it Thee."

Jesus saith unto her, "Thy brother shall rise again." Martha saith unto Him, "I know that he shall rise again in the Resurrection at the last day."

Jesus saith unto her, "I am the resurrection and the life; he that believeth in me, though he were dead, yet shall he live; and whosoever liveth and believeth in me, shall never die. Believest thou this?"

This was the trial of her faith, to which all that had passed between them, since their first acquaintance, was but a prelude. The contempt of her friends; the slights that had been cast upon the character of Christ in the past four days; His refusal to come and heal her brother, even upon her thrilling appeal, and all the distress she had endured through that bitter stroke of death, distress from which she knew He might have preserved her by a single word, all these thoughts passed rapidly across her mind, and had her faith been an ordinary one, she could not have made Him an acceptable answer. But all clouds had blown away from before her at the sight of his beloved countenance. The Being who had condescended to call her brother, Lazarus, the man of his love, who had accepted her service, and acknowledged her attachment to His person, one look from Him obliterated all despair, and made green her faith. She saith unto Him, "Yea, Lord, I believe thou art the Christ, the Son of God, which should come into the world."

And here I would point out to you an incident of this narrative, which affords us the original of the Sister's Hailing Sign. It relates to the upward glance and appealing gesture with which the sorrowing Martha, kneeling at the Saviour's feet, expressed her heavy woe and implored His sympathy.

The acknowledgment of her unswerving faith in Him, could but be pleasing to Christ. He raised her kindly by the hand and conducted her to the house; there, receiving the same tender remonstrance from Mary, He inquired where the dead man was laid, and accompanied them thither weeping.

The Sacred history instructs us that He raised Lazarus from the dead and restored him to the arms of his now joyful sisters. This, according to our traditions, was in acknowledgment of Martha's faith, which, amidst all that could oppress and discourage the mind of woman, was steadfast upon its Divine Object.

MARTHA

John XI, 26

Low in the dust she knelt,
Low at the Saviour's feet:
With weeping eyes and hands upraised
Up to the Mercy-seat:
The friendless one was sad —
Complainingly she sighed —

Oh hadst thou come while yet he lived,
  My brother had not died.

The Saviour's gentle smile
  New hope in Martha woke:
Thy brother, he shall rise again,
  The gracious Saviour spoke: —
  The living shall not die
  If in me they believe:
And though they in the dust may lie,
  The very dead shall live.

Into the Master's face
  The sister meekly gazed:
There is no fear in love, there is
  No doubt where faith is placed;
  Thou art, thou art the Christ —
  In thee the dead shall live —
Whatever thou shalt ask of God,
  I know that God will give.

Before an open tomb
  A joyful group is seen;
The grave has yielded up its dead,
  And Martha's faith is green.
  No longer tears are thine
  Sweet sister, soul of faith!
Thy love for Christ has full reward,
  Thy brother's won from death.

Sec. 7. The Fifth Degree having been conferred as described in the preceding Chapters, Heleon will address the Initiate or Initiates with the following Lecture of Electa:

My Sister:

The Evangelist John, one of the Patron Saints of Masonry, and one of the acknowledged pillars of the early Christian Church, was the successor in the Grand Mastership, of Gaius, the husband of Electa. The early Christians were much indebted to Masonry, whose principles united them together, and whose votaries often protected them from the swords of their enemies. It was to this end, that St. John was induced, at the advanced age of more than ninety years, to accept an office, requiring at that period, great prudence and discretion, and to manage its affairs even to the time of his death.

Among the converts from heathenism to the religion of a crucified Redeemer, none was more conspicuous, whether we consider her elevated rank in life, her age or her renowned benevolence, than Electa. Reared up under the principles of paganism, it was not until the age of fifty and upwards that she knew anything of Jesus. But attending from curiosity's sake the preaching of St. Paul, in one of his visits to the province in which she lived, she became converted, and, in company with her husband and all her household, professed the religion which it was his business to establish.

At that period the Christian religion was peculiarly obnoxious to the people. True, it was spreading rapidly, yet its converts were generally from the lowest classes, so that when a person from the rank in which Electa was born, was known to shock the popular prejudices by adopting it, it was at great personal hazard. Electa experienced this in full force. Her good name became an object of reproach in the common mouth, and though, from her husband's station in the Masonic Fraternity, no personal violence was attempted, yet she felt that her old age was destined to be her most painful portion, and that she was leaving a fatal legacy to her children.

Yet, her devotion to the cause of charity was rather increased than relaxed by these considerations. Her benevolence, which, even while she was a pagan, was the great passion of her life, became, now sanctified by her Christian graces, a wonderful virtue. For she labored now as the servant of One who went about doing good. Enlightened by His precepts and His example, she sought out those who were lost and ministered to them. Every grade of suffering, every class of distress, had its place in her care. Her mansion, the most splendid in the province, was made a hospital for the infirm, and a great caravansary for way-worn travelers; while her heart, larger than her dwelling in capacity for good, was the abode of every good and sympathetic feeling for the comfort of her race. And so, for fifteen years, she lived and ripened for a better world.

The time of trial of the Christian Church, the time to separate its chaff and to purge it with the fires of persecution, came at last. A law went forth from the Emperor at Rome, that all who professed the religion of Christ should be made to renounce it under penalty of death. The soldiers, those implacable persecutors of the Christians, were enjoined to execute the law in every province of the kingdom, and, without mercy, to exterminate all those suspected of holding the Christian faith, being commanded to trample upon the Cross, should they refuse to obey. This law was the signal for the most general and unrelenting attack upon the church that, up to that period, it had ever been called upon to sustain. Amongst those who fell victims to its operations was Electa.

Intelligence of this law had early reached St. John, by means of his Masonic communication with Rome. He had been put upon his guard against the impending peril, and his duties as Grand Master, conjoined with those of a Christian Apostle, prompted him, as rapidly as possible, to extend the warning to others, situated like himself. But amongst all the votaries of Christ who would become the objects of this bitter persecution, his mind reverted to none so painfully as to Electa. He had so often shared her Christian hospitality, so often pointed her out to younger converts as a model of Christian duty, that the question how she would endure this terrible trial came to his mind with great power, and he determined to go in person to her dwelling, disguised as a soldier, and, in that capacity, to deliver her the cruel message she was so soon to hear.

It was a painful day's journey, and ere he reached its end, the aged Apostle was overcome with fatigue. He reached her threshold, however, though with exceeding difficulty, and, having knocked for admission, leaned, quite exhausted, against the pillar at the entrance. She came in reply and saw him, as he stood, dust covered; his garb, old and tattered; and his appearance, that of a miserable soldier.

But such an object was to her as if sent from God. She approached him with the kindest language, assisted him to enter her house, which, she assured him, in the name of the Lord Jesus Christ, was freely open to his wants; conducted him to its best apartment, and with her own hands, as enjoined by the example of Christ, washed his feet. She refreshed him with comfort after comfort; fed him with the best food; animated him with her richest wine; filled his purse; supplied him with raiment, good and new; anticipated all his desires, and when she found there was no other demand upon her bounty, gave him good wishes and prayers, such as she might have bestowed upon him had he been her own aged father.

But now, refreshed with all these attentions, St. John, still in his capacity of a soldier, opened the business which had called him there: informed her of the cruel law passed to crush out the Church; assured her that it was the particular business of the soldier to execute the law, and that, too, in the most summary manner; and concluded by commanding her to give the names of such persons in her vicinity as were suspected of holding to the doctrines of Christ. But she made him no reply and looked him steadily in the face.

Then he declared that her silence was a cause of suspicion, and that if she had any Christians in her household, and concealed the fact, her own life would pay the forfeit. But she still answered not a word.

Speaking with great sternness to her then, he said, that her persistence in refusing to divulge these names was proof positive of her own share in this religious belief, and that her life was forfeited thereby. But, in view of her remarkable kindness to him in his distress, he offered to save her and her family, and gave her the Cross, with the command to trample it under foot. This, he said, was the test required by the law of those who should renounce Christ.

Electa received the Cross — precious emblem of that which had been stained with her Saviour's blood — and her countenance, which had all the time been fixed in a steady gaze upon him, changed into Christian tenderness and tears. She eagerly and repeatedly kissed it, and pressed it with ardor to her bosom. Then resuming her sternness and holy indignation with which she had listened to his words, she declared that, for fifteen years, she had expected and waited for such a message as this. That she was a Christian; she, her husband, her children, her servants, — and that all of them would submit as cheerfully as herself to this trial. Finally, she bade him spare her any more such offers, and to do his duty, asseverating with the strongest evidence, that God would assuredly give her grace to do hers.

This trial having been so satisfactorily sustained, St. John now revealed himself to her in his true character; told her the object of his coming and of his disguise; and exposed to her the full character of that trial, which, in a few weeks, at the most, would come upon her. At the same time he assured her of his belief that she would as satisfactorily sustain it as she had done the other, being the fairest among ten thousand and altogether lovely; and promised her that if she perished in this just cause, he would institute a Degree of Adoptive Masonry, of which her history should form the basis, and name it after her, that her name and sufferings might be perpetuated in the Masonic Fraternity while time should endure.

Ere long, the trial came. The soldiers in great numbers, visited that province. Their commander, a Mason, endeavored to save Electa, by inducing her to submit to the test, but in vain. She was, therefore, thrown into a loathsome dungeon, with her family; and her splendid mansion and possessions totally destroyed. For a twelvemonth, they were fed in that prison by the Masonic charity; then they were visited by the Judge, a humane man and a Mason, who, like the commander, proposed the test as a means of escape, still available. But it was steadfastly spurned, and though worn by sufferings, Electa begged for that one favor, that their martyrdom might not be delayed from any expectation that any of them would renounce their religion — for they never would.

They were then dragged forth and scourged nigh unto death. After this, they were taken to the top of the nearest hill and crucified. One after the other of that lovely band, Electa saw pierced with nails and hung upon the Cross to die, — last of all, she was crucified also. And as she made her expiring prayers it was remarked by them who stood by, that they were for the pardon and happiness of her cruel murderers.

True to his word, the Grand Master St. John, upon receiving intelligence of her triumphant death, made known his promise to the Fraternity in Grand Lodge assembled, and established the Degree of Electa, announcing for its sign, the CHRISTIAN'S HAILING SIGN, a remembrance of the manner of her death.

ELECTA

2 John I, 5

Her gentle smile and yielding heart
   Shall grace our world no more:
She chose the true but bitter part
   Her Saviour chose before;
The Cross its gloomy load has borne,
   The grave concealed its prey,
But in the triumph she has won
   We cast all tears away.

This heartless world but ill can spare
   Its jewels rich and few, —
But she, most excellent and rare,
   The generous and the true —
She, in departing, left to earth
   Such patterns of her faith,
That though her life was matchless worth,
   Even worthier was her death.

By her we learn, the tenderest heart
   Is bravest to endure —
For at the Cross He'll not desert
   Who all its sufferings bore;
Amongst ten thousand, fairest she,
   When bleeding, dying, high,
Her risen Lord proclaimed her free,
   And called her to the sky.

Her fame upon the wings of Time
   Through every land has swept; —
Electa's FAITH unmatched, sublime,
   Electa's NAME has kept:

> Meek, radiant one! whose willing blood
> Thy faith in Christ did seal,
> While hearts can feel and tears be stirred,
> Thy history we will tell.

Sec. 8. LECTURE UPON THE LABYRINTH

The pathway of human life meanders into the Labyrinth, and the most prudent pilgrim upon the journey fails to accomplish the plans with which he sets out. He may go swiftly and prosperously forward a little ways, but suddenly his course is checked by obstacles he does not understand, and powers that he cannot overcome. Again he attempts to move in a right line, to some new goal of his desires; again all for awhile may seem to conspire to accomplish his ends, when, unexpectedly as before, his way is stopped: and so all through his life, he drives from point to point, baffled and astonished at every turn, until, wearied and disgusted with repeated disappointments and failures, and craving something that is not subject to change and disaster, he stands, at last, before the Great Light of all, and is accosted by the Judge of the quick and dead.

Sec. 9. LECTURE ON THE ANALOGIES

To show more nearly the Christian Analogies of the traditions of our Order, observe the following:

JEPHTHAH'S DAUGHTER, to preserve the honor of her father who had sworn upon his soul to make a certain sacrifice, died to fulfill that pledge; even so Christ, to preserve the honor of God His Father, who had sworn that the soul that sinneth shall die, gave His life as a sacrifice.

RUTH forsook her native country, wealth, and friends, and dwelt in Bethlehem, for the honor of the religion she had professed; even so Christ left behind him the glory and joy of heaven, and came, a stranger, poor and lowly, to Bethlehem for the sake of religion.

ESTHER cheerfully imperiled her kingdom and her life for the love she bore to her people; even so Christ voluntarily resigned His crown and life, to save his chosen from impending and eternal death.

MARTHA, amidst the utmost gloom and despair that death can throw around humanity, maintained her faith in the Word of God; — even so Christ in every trial of His varied life, His Agony in the Garden, His Scourge and His Cross, faltered not in his reliance upon the Word of God.

ELECTA, for the love she bore her Saviour, resigned all things, — good name, wealth, family, and life itself, in Christian testimony; — even so Christ, possessing all things, gave all things even to his life itself in testimony of His ardent love for His chosen people. Was there ever love like His?

Sec. 10. LECTURE ON THE MEANS OF RECOGNITION

A Stella or Protector, offering to submit to examination, for the purpose of proving membership in this Order, will first present a "Signet of Withdrawal" from the last Constellation to which she was attached, if she have one in possession, and also her Tessera; after which the examination will proceed in the following manner, led by Warder:

Q. 1. Do you declare upon your honor as a woman (or a Master Mason as the case may be), that you have been regularly inducted into the mysteries of the American Adoptive Rite, according to the forms authorized by the Supreme Constellation thereof?

A.   I do.

Q. 2. Do you declare upon your honor as a woman, that you have not, to your own knowledge, committed any act, or neglected any duty by which you have forfeited your rights and privileges as a Stella of the American Adoptive Rite?

A.   I do.

Q. 3. Are you an Adopted Mason?

A.   * * * * * * * *

Q. 4. Why then are you come?

A.   * * * * *

The following questions relate to "the Signet of Emblems," which should be in the possession of every member of this Order.

Q. 5. To what do these five emblems allude?

A.   They allude to Jesus Christ who is the light and key of this Order.

Q. 6. Can you explain them?

A.   * * * * *

Q. 7. What is the name of the first Point of the Eastern Star?

A.   Jephthah's Daughter.

Q. 8. What is the Emblem?

A.   The Sword.

Q. 9. Can you explain it?

A.   It reminds me that, by the Sword, in the hands of her own father, was Jephthah's Daughter slain.

Q. 10. What is the color?

A.   Blue.

Q. 11. Can you explain it?

A.   It alludes to the mountains, in whose solitude Jephthah's Daughter passed two months, while preparing herself for the fate she had invoked.

Q. 12. Can you give me the Daughter's Hailing Sign? To what does it allude? Can you give me the Answering Pass? To what does it allude? (See the Tuilleur for instructions upon points not explained in this Section.)

Q. 13. What is the name of the Second Point of the Eastern Star?

A.   Ruth.

Q. 14. What is the Emblem?

A.   The Sheaf.

Q. 15. Can you explain it?

A.   It reminds me of the liberality of Boaz, who, from his sheaves, commanded that portions be taken and cast in Ruth's way, that she might gather an abundance.

Q. 16. What is the Color?

A.   Yellow.

Q. 17. Can you explain it?

A.   It alludes to the barley-field, in which Ruth was gleaning.

Q. 18. Can you give me the Widow's Hailing Sign? To what does it allude? Can you give me the Answering Pass? To what does it allude?

A.   * * *

Q. 19. What is the name of the Third Point of the Eastern Star?

A.   Esther.

Q. 20. What is the Emblem?

A.   The Crown.

Q. 21. Can you explain it?

A.   It reminds me of the queenly state of Esther, and of the manner in which she hailed the notice of the King.

Q. 22. What is the Color?

A.   White.

Q. 23. Can you explain it?

A.   It alludes to the color of her silken robes, emblematical of the spotless purity of her character.

Q. 24. Can you give me the Wife's Hailing Sign? To what does it allude? Can you give me the Answering Pass? To what does it allude?

A.   (See Tuilleur).

Q. 25. What is the name of the Fourth Point of the Eastern Star?

A.   Martha.

Q. 26. What is the Emblem?

A.   The Pillar Rent.

Q. 27. Can you explain it?

A.   It reminds me of the sudden death of Lazarus.

Q. 28. What is the Color?

A.   Green.

Q. 29. Can you explain it?

A.   It alludes to the Resurrection of Lazarus.

Q. 30. Can you give me the Sister's Hailing Sign? To what does it allude? Can you give me the Answering Pass? To what does it allude?

A.   (See Tuilleur).

Q. 31. What is the name of the Fifth Point of the Eastern Star?

A.   Electa.

Q. 32. What is the Emblem?

A.   The Clasped Hands.

Q. 33. Can you explain it?

A.   It reminds me of the ardent hospitality of Electa, excited by the view of poverty and distress.

Q. 34. What is the Color?

A.   Red.

Q. 35. Can you explain it?

A.   It alludes to the liberal spirit with which she dealt with her poorest guests.

Q. 36. Can you give me the Christian's Hailing Sign? To what does it allude? Can you give me the Answering Pass? To what does it allude?

A.   (See Tuilleur).

Q. 37. What is the cabalistic motto of the Eastern Star? Explain it, a letter for words, and a word for a sentence.

This examination being satisfactory conducted and the Memorial properly given, the party thus applying, may safely be admitted as a visitor.

Sec. 11. LECTURE ON THE SIGNET OF EMBLEMS.

The five small emblems in the center are thus explained:

They all allude to Christ, who is the Light and Key to the Eastern Star. The first, THE BIBLE AND CROSS, alludes to Christ under the title of The Word. See the motto at the bottom of the Signet. Christ is called "The Word of God," because all that we know of that great Being, in His love for us, was revealed through the Word of Christ, His Son, and is upon record for our use.

The second, THE LILY, alludes to Christ under the title of The Lily of the Valley. See the motto at the right hand side of the Signet. Christ is called "The Lily of the Valley," because as that flower is fairest in the fields of nature, so is the character of Jesus the highest in the scale of grace, purity, and beauty that can be presented us.

The third, THE SUN, alludes to Christ under the title of the Sun of Righteousness. See the motto at the lower right hand corner of the Signet. Christ is called "The Sun of Righteousness," because as the Sun is the source of heat and light to the otherwise barren earth, so hath Christ shone into our otherwise barren hearts to give us the light and warmth of His own glorious character.

The fourth, THE LAMB AND CROSS, alludes to Christ under the title of The Lamb of God. See the motto at the lower left hand corner of the Signet. Christ is called "The Lamb of God," because as the Lamb was made the object of Sacrifice in the ceremonial expiation for sin, so was Christ slain once for all, a willing victim for the sin of all who put their trust in Him.

The fifth, THE LION, alludes to Christ under the title of The Lion of the Tribe of Judah. See the motto at the left hand side of the Signet. Christ is called the "Lion of the Tribe of Judah" because as the Lion was the type of all that was great in strength, so is the Saviour of men most powerful, even Almighty.

The other mottoes around the border display other graces and qualities of Jesus Christ, as the Prince of Peace, the Star out of Jacob, the Morning Star, etc., etc., figures, in which the Scriptural writers have displayed Him as the type of all that is wise, Strong, and Beautiful.

Sec. 12. LECTURE ON THE CABALISTIC MOTTO

JEPHTHAH'S DAUGHTER, because she devoted her life to preserve her father from eternal infamy, was the * * * * * * *

RUTH, because she forsook home, friends, and all things, in a heathen land, to seek out the people of God, was the * * * * * * * *

ESTHER, because she offered her crown and life to preserve her people, was * * * * * * *

MARTHA, because amidst all the despair of death and the woe of desolation, she preserved her faith in the Word of God, was the * * * * * * *

ELECTA, because in her martyrdom for Christ's sake she hesitated not to sacrifice all things that love can prize or friendship cherish, was the * * * * * * *

(See Tuilleur.)

Sec. 13. THE SIGNS

Each sign alludes to some important historical incident in the Degree to which it belongs. The signs should be given gracefully and with precision. Each Stella should be thoroughly instructed in these highly important essentials of the Order, for without them none could correctly establish an Adoptive Claim among strangers.

The Signs are for the use of ladies, mainly. Gentlemen who have need of assistance from their brethren, will use the means appertaining to Symbolic Masonry to acquire it.

Sec. 14.   CONCLUDING REMARKS

The varied and great interests, connected with the subject of Adoptive Masonry, are now finally committed to the hands of those who are personally and chiefly concerned in their prosperity. Whoever has a beloved wife, daughter or sister — whoever is preparing to enter the marriage relation, and whoever looks with philanthropic eyes upon the interests of the wife, daughter or sister of another; these are all called upon to advance such an enterprise as this; and to such is the Adoptive Rite presented. Those who have labored zealously and without hope of pecuniary reward, to perfect it, feel an abiding confidence of its success in the hands of such men.

The Pillars of this Order must keep in careful thought this fact — that the world everywhere watches with cruel readiness to villify female character. Nothing is so easily soiled by a foul breath as female character. The very fact of a lady joining this Society, and meeting gentlemen in locked and secluded places will afford an opportunity for slander which will assuredly be seized upon unless you meet it with the proper explanations. It is by showing the character of the gentlemen who govern the Constellation, explaining the nature of the Work in which the parties unitedly are engaged, and arguing the absolute necessity of secrecy in such work, that you can best provide against, or rebut improper imputations, from whatever source.

Much interest will be added to the work and lectures, by each officer committing to memory her or his appropriate portions. This has been alluded to before; it is particularly applicable to the eloquent and instructive Lectures in this Chapter.

It is not important, nor is it particularly desirable, that the membership of a Constellation should be rapidly filled up, or that the Degrees should be conferred upon Candidates in rapid succession. As the membership of each Constellation is limited to twenty-five of each sex, it is rather recommended that not more than one or two be received at each meeting, and that applicants be only allowed one Degree at a meeting. But of this, the Pillars of the Constellation are allowed to be the proper judges. Only it should be considered that the permanent interests of Masonry are better established by getting up a desire among *outsiders* for admission than a craving among the members to increase their numbers.

Whatever physical deformities or deficiencies that would render a person incapable of giving and responding to any of the means of recognition, are a bar to initiation.

The funds in the treasury of the Constellation are never to be appropriated to the relief of males. They go to aid poor and distressed worthy females; first, those of the Adoptive Rite, afterwards those who are not.

There will, occasionally be a difficulty, possibly an insurmountable one, in ascertaining the correctness of a lady's claim to the privileges of Adoption. One whose husband, father, or brother is deceased, or far absent, may be unable to prove that for which there are ample grounds for conjecture. In such cases, the Pillars must insist on *proof*, regardless of conjecture.

The Pillars should most candidly but courteously, state to each sister, upon her initiation, (or before it if thought necessary) that in the event of the expulsion, suspension, or demitting of the gentleman through whom she is Adopted, and whose name appears with her own upon the Membership Board, that she is at once stricken from the roll, though without disgrace, and cannot be allowed any of the privileges of this Rite, until he is re-instated or re-affiliated.

Votes in a Constellation may best be taken by raised hands; this is where the ballot is not required.

The general rules, applicable to a well-understood system of Masonic Jurisprudence (see Morris' Code of Masonic Laws) and the ordinary Parliamentary regulations and usages are applicable to the government of an Adoptive Constellation.

All the furniture, paraphernalia, etc., specified in the preceding Chapters should be provided as far as practicable. Like the fittings, etc., of a Masonic Lodge, these things are part of the instruction of the System, which will be bald and barren without them. A melodeon or piano for the music is particularly recommended, as serving to throw very great interest around the ceremonies. Every member, Stella or Protector, should supply herself with a neat Tessera of a quality that will not discredit the Society, if seen by other eyes than theirs.

It is earnestly desired as vastly conclusive to the general interests of Adoptive Masonry, that its votaries should preserve for publication, all matters of interest, all valuable incidents, historical facts, etc., that show up the workings and progress of the Order. Those, particularly, who become known as its friends, in the first years of its establishment, are desired, as much for their own honor and credit, as for the general good, to consider themselves called upon to act as its historians.

It is worthy of remark here, that though a Brother Mason, not regularly inducted into this Rite, may, by coming into possession of the Mosaic Book, acquaint himself with the spirit and details of the System, yet he could not enter a Constellation, or enjoy any of those privileges of association, which constitute the very foundation of all Adoptive Masonry. To such a one, practically, the book would be of no service, even were he vile enough, which is not to be supposed of a Mason, to endeavor clandestinely to use it.

Information relative to the regalia, etc., of officers and members will be found in the general publications of the Order.

It will be observed that this Order, like the Encampment Order of Masonry, is a Christian System, and that none can consistently become its members, whether male or female, save those who at least believe in Jesus Christ.

No check or restraint should be placed upon those who may wish to withdraw their membership from this Order. But the formality of a vote of dismissal, and a candid statement of the loss of privilege thereby incurred, should never be neglected.

There is much that may, with propriety, be added both in the ceremonies and lectures of these Degrees; much that is explanatory — and in the hands of eloquent and zealous Masons it is expected that these additions will be made. The only caution necessary to be observed is, that no discrepancy be found between these addenda and the work and lectures here given.

Finally, in commencing this enterprise, let the zealous Mason be prepared to meet opposing arguments and to give a reason for the faith that is within him. The grand object is, to unite the Sisters of Masonry as its Brothers are united, and thus make the family complete. Holy and laudable motive. There are many, very many Masons, who have never themselves experienced the real benefits of Masonry, or felt its real wants; how can we expect that such will feel the necessity for this? Others have suffered from the evils of other affiliated Societies, organized in imitation of Masonry, and will be likely to confound this with those. Others are used to oppose everything they do not understand, and still others everything that is new. From all, the votary of Adoption must look for opposition and be prepared in the spirit of wisdom, and love, to overcome it. And may the Divine giver of all good increase the wisdom and extend the love to his own eternal honor and glory. Amen.

Sec. 15.　MISCELLANEOUS SONGS

THE DIRGE OF THE FREEMASON'S DAUGHTER

The green-waving willow mourns over thy tomb,
Bewailing the maiden who passed in her bloom;
And soft dews of heaven bathe lightly the bed
Where the fairest and dearest lies low with the dead.

Though fond hearts are breaking in passion from thee;
Through sorrow's wild burden thine, lost one, is free;
But where is the smile that woke riches of light?
It has faded — ah! faded — and dark is the night!

We miss thee; for nothing is left us so fair;
We miss thee; this earth has no spirit so rare;
We miss thee; we pine for the eyes and the tongue —
For the eye that was summer, the voice that was song.

The voice of thy parting swells round us again;
The acacia's bright story adds joy to the strain;
For emblems, though sad, twine with Faith, Hope and Love
With the pure in God's favor we'll meet thee above.

90

LOVE AND LIGHT, OR THE FREEMASON'S DAUGHTER

Where lies the maid, the Mason's daughter?
   Where is her tomb?
Down by the softly flowing water,
   There is her long, long home —
Sounds of the flowing water breathing
   Peace o'er her bed.
Vines in a tender sorrow wreathing
   Bowers for the Mason's dead.

CHORUS

Sister, O! farewell forever,
   None are left like thee —
Weep, Brothers! o'er the dark, dark river
   Fades "Love and Light" far away.

Oft, when the mystic toils are ended,
   True hearts among,
What joys the evening hours attended,
   Blest with her matchless song.
Thence, when the midnight chimes resounded,
   Rapt with her lay,
Each from the circle that surrounded
   Parted in cheer away.

CHORUS

When through the haunts of sorrow straying,
   At duty's call,
We, every sign of grief obeying,
   Bore friendly aid to all,
How, with us on the holy mission,
   Fervent was she!
How like a bright and blissful vision
   'Twas her delight to be!

CHORUS

Death called the Mason's daughter early,
   Far, far too soon:
Blight nipped the tender flower unfairly,

Fades her light at noon.
Doubtless in mercy it was given,
   Mercy divine,
That in the love and light of heaven
   She might forever shine.

CHORUS

Sing, every little bird around her,
   Sing o'er her tomb:
Forms from the better world have found her
   Here, where we made her home.
Grief, to this sacred scene forbidden,
   Vanish afar:
Only a little time she's hidden —
   Christ will the maid restore.

END

Thank you for buying this Cornerstone book!

For over 25 years now, I've tried to provide the Masonic community with quality books on Masonic education, philosophy, and general interest. Your support means everything to us and keeps us afloat. Cornerstone is by no means a large company. We are a small family owned operation that depends on your support.

Please visit our website and have a look at the many books we offer as well as the different categories of books.

If your lodge, Grand Lodge, research lodge, book club, or other body would like to have quality Cornerstone books to sell or distribute, write us. We can give you outstanding books, prices, and service.

Thanks again!

Michael R. Poll
Publisher
Cornerstone Book Publishers
1cornerstonebooks@gmail.com
http://cornerstonepublishers.com

More Masonic Books from Cornerstone

Masonic Enlightenment
The Philosophy, History and Wisdom of Freemasonry
Edited by Michael R. Poll
6 x 9 Softcover 180 pages
ISBN 1887560750

Morgan: The Scandal That Shook Freemasonry
by Stephen Dafoe
Foreword by Arturo de Hoyos
6x9 Softcover 484 pages
ISBN 1934935549

Illustrations of Masonry
by William Preston
Additions by George Oliver
6 x 9 Softcover 400 pages
ISBN 1613422709

Our Stations and Places - Masonic Officer's Handbook
by Henry G. Meacham
Revised by Michael R. Poll
6 x 9 Softcover 164 pages
ISBN: 1887560637

Knights & Freemasons: The Birth of Modern Freemasonry
By Albert Pike & Albert Mackey
Edited by Michael R. Poll
Foreword by S. Brent Morris
6 x 9 Softcover 178 pages
ISBN 1887560661

Robert's Rules of Order: Masonic Edition
Revised by Michael R. Poll
6 x 9 Softcover 212 pages
ISBN 1887560076

Cornerstone Book Publishers
www.cornerstonepublishers.com

More Masonic Books from Cornerstone

Documents Upon Sublime Freemasonry
by Joseph McCosh
Foreword by Michael R. Poll
6x9 Softcover 115 pages
ISBN 9781613423110

Chapter Rose Croix
by Albert Pike
Foreword by Albert Mackey
6x9 Softcover 108 pages
ISBN 1-453762-02-7

Morals and Dogma of the Scottish Rite Craft Degrees
by Albert Pike
foreword by Michael R. Poll
6x9 Softcover 152 pages
ISBN 1-887560-86-6

1849 Masonic Address of John Gedge, M.W.G.M. of the Louisiana Grand Lodge of Ancient York Masons
Includes:
The Elimination of the French Influence in Louisiana Masonry
by Michael R. Poll
Softcover 61 pages
ISBN 1-9781613423141

The Masonic Pageant
The Scottish Rite Degrees of the Supreme Council, NMJ
by Frank Conway
Foreword by Christopher L. Hodapp
7.5 x 9.25 Softcover 330 pages
ISBN: 1934935921

Cornerstone Book Publishers
www.cornerstonepublishers.com

More Masonic Books from Cornerstone

The History of Magic
by Eliphas Levi
Translated by Arthur Edward Waite
6x9 Softcover 594 pages
ISBN 1613421559

An Esoteric Reading of Biblical Symbolism
by Harriet Tuttle Bartlett
6x9 Softcover 232 pages
ISBN 1613420803

The Turba Philosophorum
by Arthur Edward Waite
6x9 Softcover 226 pages
ISBN: 1613422091

The Initiates of the Flame
by Manly P. Hall
6x9 Softcover 96 pages
ISBN 1613421990

The Symbolism of Colour
by Ellen Conroy
6x9 Softcover 80 pages
ISBN 1613420838

Isis Unveiled
*A Master-Key to the Mysteries of Ancient
and Modern Science and Theology*
by H.P. Blavatsky
6x9 Softcover 2 volume set 1,374 pages
ISBN 978-1-61342-298-4

Cornerstone Book Publishers
www.cornerstonepublishers.com

New Orleans Scottish Rite College

http://www.youtube.com/c/NewOrleansScottishRiteCollege

Clear, Easy to Watch
Scottish Rite and Craft Lodge
Video Education

Made in the USA
Monee, IL
17 September 2022

14161373R00073